ADULTHOOD

for

BEGINNERS

ADULTHOOD

for

BEGINNERS

All The Life Secrets

Nobody Bothered to Tell You

ANDY BOYLE

A TarcherPerigee Book

tarcherperigee

An imprint of Penguin Random House LLC
375 Hudson Street
New York, New York 10014

Most TarcherPerigee books are available at special quantity discounts for bulk purchase for sales promotions, premiums, fund-raising, and educational needs. Special books or book excerpts also can be created to fit specific needs. For details, write: SpecialMarkets@penguinrandomhouse.com.

ISBN 9780143130512

Printed in the United States of America
1 3 5 7 9 10 8 6 4 2

Book design by Sabrina Bowers

For my mom and dad,
the main reason I know anything.

Contents

DATING AWESOMENESS

WORK AWESOMENESS

BODY AWESOMENESS

NEXT-LEVEL AWESOMENESS

Introduction

DEAR HUMAN OR LITERATE CAT,

This is an advice book. You're right to ask, "Why should I listen to this guy's advice? He doesn't even have a good haircut." Correct, and ouch, my barber's doing the best he can. The only qualifications I have for writing an advice book is I've lived a few decades, I've failed a lot, and I don't want you to make the same mistakes as me. This book is a collection of the advice I wish I'd had when I was younger. I've gained it through years of awkwardness, mistakes, and, wow, a lot of bad dates. This book should act like some cheat codes for your life, allowing you to level up quicker, avoiding some pratfalls, hopefully while giggling along the way.

A bit about me: I'm a journalist, more or less. I'm not qualified to be that, either, but people keep letting me do it. I initially started college by majoring in vocal music performance, proof your parents shouldn't always let you follow your dreams. But I fell into writing for a living, working for my college newspaper, then bigger newspapers, then making websites, then giving talks at colleges and workshops. Then on the side I started doing stand-up comedy and improv, and writing funny things for money and so much more. Lots of failure along the way.

This book happened because I've reinvented myself a few times. One thing I did was I went from being a balding, fat, and fun party drunk young professional to a skinnier and healthier nondrinking older professional. (Now featuring less hair!) I wrote a blog post near the end of 2015 detailing what I learned not drinking for two years. And in a tale as old as time, it went crazy viral. (The same thing happened to Jane Austen.) It ran in newspapers, all over the Internet, even on the *Today* show's website. (Hi, Matt Lauer!)

Months prior to my viralness, I wrote an early version of this book. I told myself I would try to get it published after I finished my mystery novel about a former stockbroker turned vampire who goes back to his hometown to find his missing sister during his ten-year high school reunion. (Yes it's as awesome as it sounds.) Because if there's anyone you want advice from, it's the guy who came up with that convoluted plot.

Then, during my virality period (which sounds like something from the Dark Ages) a second tale as old as time happened: A fantastic editor reached out, asking me about this advice book I mentioned writing in my viral blog post. (Just like Jane Austen!) Now, many months later, here we are. A book of advice exists and you're reading it *right now*!

In this book, you'll hear a bunch of advice about life, love, happiness, health, dating, careers, hobbies, and not looking like a dumbass. I especially excel at the latter, because if anyone's looked regularly like a dumbass and learned from it, it's me. Here's a quick list of my biggest moments of awkwardness:

- I was once hired to give a talk at a college and they had some delicious food for the speakers. I complimented the hosts on their "deep-dish egg pizza." They informed me the correct term is quiche. They didn't book me a second time.

- By accident I once called a boss "Mom." This boss was also a man.

- A woman once broke up with me after seeing me at the grocery store. She had her new boy toy in tow and was like, "Oh! By the way."

- In college I wrote a sex advice column once, about dealing with your dorm neighbors having loud conjugal relations, in which I referred to sex as the "potato toss."

- I once was so fat I ripped my pants in the middle of a meeting at the eighth largest newspaper in America and then fixed those pants with duct tape.

See? I'm a normal human, like you! Also, it's important I mention this: I am a white heterosexual cis dude raised by two loving middle-class Midwestern parents, so I definitely see the world through that privileged lens. I've tried to check that privilege whenever possible, but I know I've made mistakes with that because I'm not perfect (yet). Regardless, the advice in these pages should still be helpful to anyone trying to figure shit out. Or who's attempting to understand someone who's trying to figure shit out. (Hello, parents!)

This book is mostly about one big idea: We all fail a lot, and then we learn from it, and that's okay! Hopefully you can learn from my soul-crushing fumbles and jump ahead to the nifty parts of life, without having to spend almost a decade, like I did, just kind of treading water in the ocean of early adulthood.

Lastly, even if you think this advice is awful, I wrote a bunch of jokes. At the very least, I hope you laugh. I know I did while writing this.

Good luck. I believe in you.

—ANDY BOYLE
Dictated but not read

A Few Things Before
We Get Started

I BELIEVE IN SOME STUFF THAT INFLUENCES MY THINKING THROUGH- out this book. So you need to know where I'm coming from before we begin. Because all this shit is true. If you disagree, that's fine. But you're wrong.

1. Regardless of your past, you can always change yourself for the better.
2. Everyone makes mistakes and you shouldn't be supershitty to people because of it.
3. Most people are assholes before they turn twenty-five, so you should forgive them for most of their dumbness.
4. Privilege is a real thing and you should be aware of your own.
5. It's not cool to be a dick to people.
6. You should give a shit about everything you do.
7. You don't get to tell someone how they should look.
8. Your opinions don't matter more than anyone else's, regardless of how important you think you may be. Or even if you get a book deal and your name is Andy Boyle.
9. Life is a science experiment, so you should constantly be making and testing hypotheses.
10. Always work toward educating yourself further.
11. Treat people *better* than you want to be treated.
12. We're all going to die someday, so make this life matter.

Okay, let's begin.

INNER
Awesomeness

Your Life's a Science Experiment

HERE'S HOW SCIENCE WORKS: PEOPLE MAKE A HYPOTHESIS, THEY create a control group, then they test that idea against the control group, and they study the results. It's the scientific method, and it's how you should be living your life.

By this I mean if you think something in your life sucks, you should change it and see if it gets better. You should always be making experiments and testing the results. Life is all about course correction. You've got a lot of time to fix things that aren't working out. But you can't start fixing them unless you first identify the problem, create a hypothesis, test it, record your data, and look back on it.

> *If you think something in your life sucks, you should change it and see if it gets better.*

MY FIRST BIG SCIENCE EXPERIMENT

At the tail end of 2013, I decided to take a break from drinking.

I planned on doing it for only a month. It was an experiment. I was looking for a way to kick-start not only my productivity, but also my general well-being.

How would my life change if I took out one of the constants of my world? I wouldn't know unless I tried it. The next chapter is from a blog post I wrote two years later. It's since become the most read article on the *Chicago Tribune*'s website. It got me on a bunch of television and radio shows. It helped create this book.

So it's only fair I tell you about the first big adulthood experiment I've ever undertaken. And what the data ended up showing me. (Spoiler alert: It was a good idea.)

> **_Who Knew:_** _In one of history's first science experiments, a guy in 240 BCE determined the Earth's circumference. I assume he used the world's first, and largest, tape measure._

What I Learned Not Drinking for Two Years

(Blog Post, Dec. 28, 2015)

TWO YEARS AGO TODAY I LAST GOT SHITHOUSED. IT WAS THE CLOS-ing night of the Lincoln Lodge, a fantastic comedy venue in Chicago in the back of a now-closed diner. It has since moved, but after that show, I thought I should take a breather from drinking—and eating meat—and focus on productivity.

Here's a short list of what I've accomplished since I stopped drinking two years ago:

- Lost 75 pounds
- Bought a badass loft condo
- Finished the first draft of an advice book
- Started exercising three days a week, then four
- Went from a size XXL to size L
- Performed in three comedy festivals
- Got a badass new job
- Finished multiple drafts of multiple television and movie scripts
- Went from a forty-two-inch waist to thirty-six inches
- Went from hating myself daily to relatively enjoying myself

A lot of this is what I externally accomplished, what I can show on paper. But I think that last one is the most important.

I've learned a lot in two years, so I thought I'd share that with you, in case you'd like to take a break from the booze cruise. Also, that's what I tell myself: I've taken a break. Maybe I'll drink again. Maybe I won't.

But overall, life seems to be a shitload better for me because I took a break. Perhaps it could be for you, too.

THINGS I'VE LEARNED

1. You don't have to drink to have fun

What a shocker! As someone who's been drinking since his senior year of high school (sorry, Mom, we weren't just "hanging out" in the basement), most events in my life revolved around booze.

Almost everything does: comedy shows, concerts, after-work functions, meetups, dates, conferences, dinner, museum tours. But guess what? The events don't change if you decide not to drink!

You're still you. Maybe you're a little less of a party animal, but is that altogether terrible? I've found that when I hang out with folks who have been drinking, I start to feel the same way I was—in terms of becoming silly, goofy, fun—when I was around people while drinking.

And I remember everything that happened during the events, too, which is always nice.

2. You have way less regrets

Since I stopped drinking, I've yet to wake up and look at my phone, see something I texted, and go, "Ugh, wwwwwwhhhhhy." I'm in control of my actions basically all of the time.

I think a lot more before I respond to something someone says. If I'm angry, it gives me time to calm down instead of just reacting like a shithead. Drinking definitely helped my inner asshole come out a lot more often.

Now I am better at keeping the jerkier side of me locked up. It still comes out, sure, but at least I have more control over when that happens.

3. People will judge the shit out of you

This one was the weirdest one to deal with. Many, many folks will give you shit for not drinking. Here are some actual things I've been told:

"C'mon, dude, just have one beer! It's not like you're going to meetings or whatever!"

"I can't trust someone who doesn't drink."

"You're not fun unless you're drunk."

"When you don't drink, it makes me feel bad about myself, which makes me not like you."

"I can't date someone who doesn't want to get drunk with me, sorry."

I bet I said some of these things back when I used to drink. Because when you're around someone who doesn't do something you like doing, you can be taken aback by it.

I've had friends who've stopped hanging out with me because I don't drink anymore. I've had relationships end (or not even start) because of it. I have been sent screenshots of people I know talking smack about me to other people because I choose to not do a thing.

It's weird. But it makes you realize the bad relationship with booze other folks must be having. And for that, I have empathy. And I hope they figure it out.

4. You sleep so much better

I haven't slept this great since before high school. Holy shit, it's fantastic. I could link you to all the studies that show how alcohol affects your sleep, but hey, take my word for it.

5. You get less sad

I don't know if I have depression, but I used to get bummed out a lot. Days where I wouldn't want to leave my apartment, or see anyone, mostly because I hated myself.

I don't hate myself nearly as much as I used to. I'm generally okay with my life and who I am. Positivity is my go-to emotion, even when something bad or terrible happens to me.

It's like I flipped this switch inside my brain: Instead of going to shittiness, I try to find the reason something is positive. It's definitely weird to have this happen to me.

6. You develop more empathy for others

A few weeks ago, this guy blared on his horn because I was crossing at a crosswalk and he wanted to turn, and he almost hit me with his car, then he flipped me off and told me to go fuck myself and die.

Old me probably would've stood in front of him, not moved, taken a photo or video of him, shared it on the Internet, explained, "Hey, look at this asshole who tried to hit me with his car!" and felt smug and wonderful about it.

Instead, after an initial moment of fear and anger, I realized, This dude is probably having an awful day. Maybe he's late for an appointment. Maybe he's trying to get to the hospital to see his sick son who has cancer. Maybe he didn't have as loving a set of parents as I did, and that's filled him with resentment his entire life.

Either way, that guy has something going on, and I wanted him to be happier. Then I felt weird, because my brain has been wired forever to be a little shit to anyone who wrongs me. But now? I generally jump to empathy. I like that it does that now.

7. You save so much money

I bought a condo. I'd like to pretend as though it wasn't because of how much money I saved not drinking and buying food while drunk, but probably one-fourth of my down payment came from just abstaining from booze.

Yeah. I know.

8. You get tired earlier

It's pretty hard for me to stay up past eleven p.m. most nights, even on the weekends. When I was drinking, booze was a magical fuel that kept me going, trying to find a new adventure.

Now that I don't drink, I'm not constantly searching for adventure, trying to find one more fun thing that will fill the empty void inside of me. I'm content with what I've done for the day, and my body wants to go to bed. I dig that.

9. You become amazingly productive

When you're not spending most of your free time at bars, you get a lot of shit done. I read more. I write more. I learn more.

I spend more time working on bettering myself and my skills than I ever would have sitting at a bar, chatting with a buddy or two. I'm much less social than I was previously, but I'm also creating more art and failing a lot more than ever before.

■ ■ ■

In the end, I know I'm going to die. I'd rather there be a few things of me still hanging around a few years after I'm dead, some sort of expression of myself that others can enjoy. That requires me to put in the time to work on projects, make something tangible and real for others to enjoy.

That seems, now, like a better use of my time than chatting with some pals at a bar. That conversation may have been great, sure, but in the end, it dies with me and those people. If I can create a few things that last longer than me, it makes my life last longer. It would mean I mattered a little more.

I'm glad I haven't been drunk for two years. Sure, I've done a few shots of Malört with people who've never tried it. And that one time a dude threatened to kick my ass if I didn't drink that shot of whiskey he bought me to congratulate me on "being so funny" after hearing me tell jokes about how I don't drink anymore.

If you ever think, hey, this drinking thing isn't fun anymore, it's okay to take a break. I just quit. For me, it's been relatively easy, and I know it isn't easy for everyone. But just know I've found countless rad people who can have fun without booze. And you can, too.

Good luck.

> **_Hot Take:_** *Because of this blog post I became mildly famous for not doing a thing. Soon I hope to become even more famous for not dating a Kardashian, not dropping a hot mix tape, and not going to the Moon.*

The Asshole Test

I DISCOVERED THE ASSHOLE TEST BY ACCIDENT WHEN I WAS TWENTY.
I was working at my college newspaper. One afternoon we were gabbing about nothing in particular. A coworker mentioned an event in the news, probably something stupid George W. Bush had done (this would be a long list).

Without thinking, I responded to the dumb thing I heard: "Wow, that's so gay."

Yup. I know. *I know.* I had gay friends; I didn't think ill toward the LGBTQ community. But I was young. I had picked up terrible behaviors from my small Nebraska town, where bigotry is kind of the norm. (If you're reading this and are from my small Nebraska town, oh goodness I'm not talking about you. Uh, I'm talking about, like, the other people. You're great!) Writing this now makes me cringe so much. But back then, it just flew out of my mouth, just like saying, "That's rad."

No one said anything after I made the homophobic remark. People just moved on. A few minutes later, a coworker came over and asked if I had a second. She took me into the hall, smiled, and asked me, "It's okay if you do, but I just wanted to know: Do you think gay people are equal to straight people?"

I was surprised at this, and had no clue why she was asking me what seemed like a silly question.

"Uh, yeah," I said. "Obviously they are."

She continued: "Okay, do you think gay people are bad at all?"

"Of course not!" I said, rolling my eyes. What was wrong with her?

She nodded. "And do you think their rights should be protected and they should be treated just like everyone else?"

"Definitely, one hundred percent."

My coworker thought for a moment, then said, "When you say something like 'that's so gay,' you're basically saying gay people, their very existence, is negative. Because you're essentially saying 'that sucks' or 'that's lame.' And it seems like you think gay people don't suck and should be treated equally."

I got defensive and felt my face get red. "It's just a word," I said.

She calmly put her hand up. "And words have meaning. They can hurt. Kids kill themselves because they've been ridiculed based on their sexual orientation. It seems like you weren't previously educated on your use of the word, which is fine, because many aren't. But now you have been."

She let that sink in before continuing: "With that education you get to choose whether or not you want to be an asshole. And I believe you don't want to be an asshole."

With that, she walked away. I sat on a couch and stewed, thinking she was full of shit. I could say whatever words I wanted! This was all so stupid. Then, thinking I was justified in my idiocy, I messaged a few friends online. They said the same thing she did, summed up as, "Yeah, you're an asshole if you still say something after being told it's mean."

· If everyone says what you're doing makes you look like an asshole, they're not wrong. I didn't want to hurt others, and it was easy to modify my behavior. Words *can* hurt. I should know—I was bullied throughout grade school and into junior high. I regularly saw therapists because of how awful it was. An asshole is basically a bully, and I was acting like one by refusing to acknowledge what my words could do to others.

> *If everyone says what you're doing makes you look like an asshole, they're not wrong.*

While I understood the Asshole Test at a basic level, it wasn't until I decided to fix myself that I completely implemented it into my life.

■ ■ ■

The test is simple: If a lot of people tell you what you're doing makes you look like an asshole, especially when it comes to the treatment of others, then you're being an asshole. If you're doing something that you would think someone else is an asshole for doing, you're being an asshole. The Asshole Test is accurate 99 percent of the time. And one should always err on the side of asshole probabilities.

That's it. If you do something and it pisses a bunch of people off, odds are you were wrong. You should apologize and learn to not do it again. Or, if you're lucky enough to have time before doing something you *think* may make you look like an asshole, check with your friends first.

Ask them, "Hey, if I do this, is that cool?" If you ask five of your pals and they all go, "Holy fuck, that would make you look like an asshole," then you have your answer. Don't do it. Your close friends are an extension of you, so if they think something is bad, so should you. (Unless your friends are dicks. But there's a later chapter in this book on that, too.)

Yes, you can sometimes make people mad because you're standing up for an injustice. Or because you're being mistreated. Or, perhaps, you're pointing out how *they* are being the asshole. Those instances are generally just fine. But for your everyday interactions with humanity, if a lot of people think you're mistreating someone, you probably are.

People sometimes have a few thoughts about the Asshole Test, so let's go through them point by point.

■ "But I'm just telling it like it is!" Usually no one asked you to tell them anything. "Telling it like it is" is actually just your interpretation of how it is. Every single time this is your justification for saying something rude or mean, you're an asshole.

- "I'm just playing devil's advocate!" So you're arguing for a side you don't agree with, just to get a rise out of someone and try to make them feel bad, even though you *actually agree with them*? That sounds like an asshole.

- "Someone else said it and *they* don't get in trouble." If your defense is to say you shouldn't be viewed negatively because someone else did that same negative thing, you're an asshole.

- "Excuse me, in this country we have *First Amendment rights*." Yes, we do! Part of those rights includes dealing with the repercussions of what you say. If you speak uncool words, people are allowed to point it out, using more speech, about your uncoolness. If you have to use the First Amendment to defend yourself for saying something despicable that's intended to hurt someone, you're an asshole.

Err on the side of not being an asshole.

When in doubt, err on the side of not being an asshole. That's how you stop being one.

Why Do We Act like Assholes?

ONE TIME WHEN I WAS IN FIRST GRADE, DURING RECESS A KID TOOK
my glasses off and snapped them in half. As he handed them back
to me, he said, "If you tell anyone I did this, everyone will say you
made it up." Then he ran off to play soccer or further develop his so-
ciopathic tendencies.

That's one of my first memories of grade school. And it was
someone making me feel awful about myself by bullying me. Getting bullied teaches you how to be a bully. It also makes you inse-
cure, makes you hate yourself, makes you think you deserved the
punishment you received. This is all bullshit, of course, but it took
me almost two decades to figure it all out. But even though it's
bullshit, it makes you want to lash out and hurt others.

Most people who act like assholes do it because they feel terrible about themselves.

Assholes think if they make others feel awful, it brings everyone down to their level. So even if you, the bully, feel bad, at least
others feel bad with you. Then you're not alone. Because insecurity
makes you feel like the loneliest person on the planet.

That insecurity also makes you think if you attack others, you'll
make yourself seem bigger by comparison. It's like that age-old
prison advice: On your first day, pick a fight with the biggest person. Even if you lose, people will think you're a bad motherfucker
and they won't start shit with you.

It's shitty. But you can learn to stop doing that.

You Gotta Love Yourself

OUR ENTIRE ECONOMY IS BASED ON MAKING YOU FEEL BAD SO YOU WILL BUY stuff. That's how advertising works. It bullies your brain into thinking you won't be cool unless you buy this brand of deodorant or drink a "True American" beer from a company owned by Belgians.

It tells you that these models on television, who are aberrations of nature and beauty in the first place, look exactly how you should look. Not only that, you can partially achieve that joy by purchasing their sixty-two-dollar-a-pair underwear. (I'll never understand why something your pee and poo can get on should cost so damn much money, but that's also why I don't sell expensive undies.)

In my thirty years, I've bought a lot of junk. I've tried to make myself look more like those sexy television models. None of it has filled that void inside of me, the void we all have. It's that nagging insecurity that says you're not good enough.

Partially, I think that voice is evolutionary. It's meant to keep propelling you forward, to get better at things, to keep you striving toward being alive. But for some of us, it bogs you down and makes you feel like crap. You can fix it and make the voice become more of a whisper, but it takes time. Here are some great steps to take toward loving yourself.

DAILY *I AM AWESOMES*

This is going to sound like hippie shit, but it works. My older sister used to have this sticker on her bathroom mirror. Whenever you looked at yourself, underneath your smiling face it would say, "YOU

ARE A SUCCESS." I used to think it was stupid. But now I realize it's such a smart idea. I call them Daily *I Am Awesomes*. (Because you *are* awesome! See? Doesn't reading that sentence feel great?)

When you compliment yourself, you internalize those things. Look at yourself in the mirror every morning and give yourself some adulation. Just because it's coming from yourself doesn't mean it won't feel good. It seems silly as hell at first, to stare at your sleepy-eyed face in the morning and go, "You're awesome and I love you."

But after you do it for a few days, man, it feels fantastic. I love looking at myself and saying nice things. I bet my cat is, like, "Oh, wow, Andy's *finally* lost it." It works, despite what my fur ball Tiberius thinks.

NO MORE NEGATING YOURSELF

I used to write lots of mean jokes about myself on Facebook. The jokes always went like this:

Hey, folks, I attempted to do this thing and I failed at it, lol. Wow, I'm twenty-eight and a failure.

Some call it underbragging. I call it just being shitty to yourself. Just like how complimenting yourself can help you feel better, constantly saying mean things to yourself (or about yourself to others) can do the opposite. Even when you're texting friends, stop calling yourself names or blaming yourself or beating yourself up.

ACCEPT WHO YOU ARE

I'm balding. I know, you would've never guessed that because my writing seems so sexy and confident. But it's a fact. Other than hiring whoever did the magical job on the heads of Joel McHale and Elon Musk, I've learned to accept this is what's happening to me.

Because of that, I don't try for fancy haircuts. That would be like looking at a burning house and saying it needs a new paint job. But I'm fine because I've accepted that.

If I don't look exactly like some hunk on *The Bachelor*, people will still like me. Same goes for you. (Attention, producers of *The Bachelor*, call me. I'd love to pitch my TV show that's *The Bachelor* except it's me choosing between cute pets to adopt. Each episode I just cuddle with cats and dogs. I guarantee huge ratings and at least a 30 percent share.)

Some parts about yourself you can't change. But those are what make you different from everyone else. That's what makes you beautiful and awesome.

KNOW EVERYONE MAKES MISTAKES

One reason I think it's hard to learn to love yourself is we live in this culture that pretends as if no one has ever fucked up. Ever. As I write this, a guy is running for president whose whole campaign thus far is, "I am the greatest and have never failed." So many people buy into these bullshit lies about others; and then they think that if they've ever made a mistake—like tripping in front of the cool kids in high school, or listening to a band people think is lame, or maybe even going into a profession and later realizing you hate it—they're the worst.

It's not true. We all make mistakes. It's literally how you get better and find success. No one just wakes up and has everything handed to them. (Unless you're the aforementioned guy running for president, or many other Rich White Men.) You gotta work at it.

Even when you're learning a new skill. *Of course* you suck when you start out! That's the whole point. But if you keep trying at it, you'll get better. Even if you're learning to love yourself better, you'll become more skilled at that, too. Trust me.

IT TAKES TIME

I hated myself for years. Because I hated myself, I didn't want to work to further myself. It kept me from pursuing anything I wanted to succeed at. "You suck, so why try?" I would tell myself. It was only after I started switching myself from negative to positive that my brain started to catch up.

After I started liking myself, it made me want to get even better at things. I wanted to get in better shape so I could dress nicer. I wanted to work more at writing because I liked what I had to say (sometimes). I pushed myself further than I had before in everything, because I was starting to *believe in myself.* (Insert the *Rocky* theme song here.)

It still sneaks in sometimes. You don't switch your brain overnight. But I'm better more often than not. That's what matters.

Pro Tip: *The evil queen in Snow White is an example of saying positive affirmations into a mirror backfiring.*

Empathy, or Why
Nickelback Fans Are the Best

HAVING EMPATHY TOWARD OTHERS AND THEIR PROBLEMS IS THE best thing you can do for yourself. Which sounds weird: How does giving a shit about others help me?

When you start to think of everyone else as worthy of your love, it furthers the thought that everyone is worthy of love, *including yourself.* If you are pushing yourself to love others, you'll love yourself in return. On top of that, loving others is a great default mode to be in.

When I was younger, I spent a lot of time judging everyone around me. It made me feel superior, because I was superinsecure, and putting others down means you are pushing yourself up. It's just like when someone makes a joke about people who like Nickelback, as if those people suck because they like a certain band. Despite owning two Nickelback albums when I was younger, I started to think anyone who liked them totally sucked. Society told me I should hate Nickelback and their fans. Because they weren't "cool." Or something.

Now I know Nickelback brings shitloads of joy to millions of people. Why the hell would I judge something that brings so much happiness to others? They're just like me, people with hopes, with dreams. People who just wanna rock, in this case to a curly-haired Canadian. What's wrong with that? Not a goddamn thing.

Also, do you know how hard it must be to love Nickelback? Everyone shits on you constantly. *Nonstop.* And yet, they decide their love for this band is worth all the stigma that goes along with it. That's such a high level of badassery.

If the world could be more like Nickelback fans, we'd all be better. So here's a few ways to love one another, just like you're a Chad Kroeger aficionado.

■ **To love others, you need to see yourself in them.** Whenever you want to lash out at someone because they're different, realize you both have something in common. You both probably had parents. Or went to school. Or awkwardly tried to make out with someone when you were fifteen. You're not as different as you think. If all else fails, you're both human. So you have that in common.

■ **You need to know they have flaws, just like you.** Nobody's perfect. Someone different from you may seem flawed because they aren't like you, but then again, *nobody is just like you.* So stop automatically cataloging people because of the "wrong" things about them. That's their life, and their choices, and you should accept them for it. Because the fact that they're different from you is what's allowed *you* to be unique.

■ **They have feelings, just like you.** The Golden Rule works pretty well in most situations: Treat people the way you'd like to be treated. Do it because they get hurt the same way you do. The opposite is true: They also can be happy. Isn't it better if your actions make people happy instead of sad? I think so.

■ **You don't know what they've been through.** I was shopping at a grocery store when a guy behind me started acting incredibly impatient. I was just buying a few items, and his cart had about the same, but you could tell he was pissed. He kept looking at me, throwing his hands up, sighing and muttering things under his breath. I was moving just as fast as humanly possible, but it wasn't enough for this man. At first I thought, "That guy is an *asshole.*" Then I realized I didn't know what was going on in his life.

Maybe his mom was sick at the hospital, and he was rushing to see her, to bring her the things he was buying. Maybe his wife just told him that morning she wanted a divorce. Maybe he just got laid off. He was going through *something* that was causing him to act that way. And maybe he was like that all the time—which must be a hard way to live. He was hurting. Just like I hurt. So my hater brain turned around, and I filled up with empathy. And I thought, "Man, I hope his day gets better." Because I did.

■ **When you're nicer to others, others are nicer to you.** When you treat everyone with respect and love, you'll see it in return. It's not a one-for-one kind of treatment. And you also shouldn't do it *because* people will be nice in return. Being loving should be its own reward. But it's true that people prefer being around folks who are easier to deal with. It's also true that if you develop a reputation for being kind, that's better than developing one for being nasty.

More opportunities come my way now because I've made a conscious effort at expressing kindness toward everyone. It's just how the universe works, I think. The nicer you are in aggregate, the nicer it is to you. The more times you go out of your way, just a little bit, to be helpful to someone, the more likely someone will do that for you.

■ **Start saying positive things in your mind about people.** When you see someone and your brain starts getting judgmental on them, just think of something positive about them. Anything. Think, "He's got a nice hat!" or, "I bet she's awesome at basketball," or maybe even, "I bet she calls her parents a lot. How nice." Start replacing the negative thoughts in your brain with something positive. When you start doing it enough times, it becomes the default. So instead of your hater brain taking over, the loving mind becomes the default.

Whenever you want to judge someone because they're different, just remember the Nickelback fans, and repeat to yourself: This is how you remind me of what I really am.

On guilty pleasures: There's no such thing as a guilty pleasure. If you like something, it's a pleasure. Including Nickelback. Anyone trying to make you feel bad for liking something that brings you joy is an asshole, so their opinions shouldn't matter. You should never feel bad for liking anything. Unless, uh, it's little kids.

There's no such thing as a guilty pleasure.

Who Knew: The first song I learned on guitar was Nickelback's "Leader of Men," so if I ever change careers and become a rock god, I'm thanking them on my Best Of album.

It's Okay to Get Sad

I GET THE SADS A LOT. IT'S HARDWIRED INTO YOUR BRAIN TO FEEL depressed sometimes. If you're always running upbeat and happy, occasionally you have to crash. But knowing the crashes *will* happen and they *will* end is what's important.

THE SADS DON'T HAVE TO LAST FOREVER

I have a few friends who like to revel in their depression. Like, they *love* feeling shitty. They romanticize it and pretend that feeling awful is how they become creative. To me, that's a bummer way to go through life, because it makes your brain get used to that feeling of dread and shittiness. That's bad.

It can become routine to feel awful. When your body gets into routines, it's hard to get out of them. So you need to tell yourself this whenever you get bummed out: "This is happening right now, but that doesn't mean it'll happen forever. Eventually I will get through this."

OTHERS GET SAD, TOO

Social media makes us think everyone is having a great time always. If you go on Instagram, not only do all your friends seem like they're the most beautiful creatures to ever wear jeans, but also they're having the most kick-ass times. Sadness never enters their world! Look at this guacamole sandwich I'm eating! Isn't life always and forever a joy?

That's not true. We all get sad. But I think because of the way

26

we're rewarded on social media, everyone acts like they're happy all the time. The biggest posts you see in your feed are someone announcing something happy. If someone posts a photo of their baby bump, 782 likes. If they Instagram the first kiss from their wedding, 1,892,732 likes. But a post that says, "Hey, you know what? Life is kind of a struggle most days, and I'm feeling pretty terrible about myself today," will be lucky to get three likes.

Social media makes it really easy to compare your whole life to someone else's highlight reel. The world now is in this constant positivity bubble, which I think has some good aspects. Because more people are trying to make their lives seem happier and more fun, they're probably focusing less, at least publicly, on all the negativity in the world. That's kind of dope. But it makes many of us, myself included, feel alone when we get a case of the sads. When I get down in the depression dumps, it seems as though nobody else ever goes through it. Maybe that's because I've curated my social media friends to a more chipper group. Maybe that's because of how the algorithms work to give me happier content. In spite of that, it sometimes makes me feel *worse* for being sad.

> *Social media makes it really easy to compare your whole life to someone else's highlight reel.*

FEELING SAD IS OKAY

It's normal. It helps make you human. Getting sad makes you realize how awesome it is to be happy. You can't have the sweet without the sour. (I totally stole that line from 2001's *Vanilla Sky,* one of Cameron Crowe's lesser-known but way great films. Go watch it. It'll give you a serious case of the sads. And then you should watch *The Lego Movie,* which is a prescription-strength drug for joy.)

So whenever you don't feel great, but it seems as though

everyone on social media is having the goddamn greatest days of their fucking lives, just remember they get sad, too. They're just not publicly writing about it. They're keeping it guarded, for whatever reason. That doesn't make them wrong. It also doesn't make you wrong for feeling the way you do. It's just how it is.

IMPORTANT NOTE: *If you've tried to get better, though, and you still feel shitty, you may be depressed. Professional help exists for a reason, and you should use it if the ideas in this chapter, or any other ideas you find, don't help. I've gotten mental health help from trained professionals at many different stages of my life. Not everyone can "just get over" being sad, as some people may say, because not everyone pulls out of sadness on their own. It's normal, so if you feel like you need outside help, you should seek it.*

YOU CAN TAKE STEPS TOWARD HAPPINESS

I'm happy that I get sad. Because it reminds me that I'm alive and that I hurt and still have the ability to feel pain. You want that. It keeps you motivated and working toward bettering yourself.

But I also know when I get down in the dumps, I can do things to make my situation better. Or at least speed up the chances that I'll get back to happy land. Here are some of my favorites:

- **Listen to Paula Abdul's "Forever Your Girl."** This is one of the greatest and peppiest pop songs of all time. It is scientifically impossible to listen to this and not want to dance your ass off. Music that makes you wanna boogie is music that affects your mind in such a positive way you gotta get it out through the power of song. If Paula can't do it for you, most modern pop music probably can.

- **Go for a walk on a sunny day.** I live in Chicago, and sunny days don't exist for months at a time. It's an Illinois state law. But whenever the weather is beautiful (defined as not a blizzard or raining or deathly hot), I like to just aimlessly explore neighborhoods and see what's in the world. Trees and greenery and blue skies put my mind at ease. Even when I'm thinking through tough problems about my life, enjoying the liveliness of the outdoors shifts my brain into a happier mode almost every time.

- **Exercise.** Walking is good exercise. So is running. Or lifting weights. Or doing jumping jacks and a few push-ups. Making your body move and exert some extra force releases endorphins that'll pop your brain into a more chipper gear. Ever since I first tried out weight lifting, my mood has always been brighter immediately after I've clanged those barbells around.

- **Have coffee with friends.** We're social creatures. Even though you may work a job where you see people every day, you're not always close to them. So make time for your friends and get together to just gab, and maybe do a little bitching and complaining. Getting together to hear how someone has been lately always makes me feel better.

- **Create something.** The artistic process certainly has its drawbacks, but *making* art always puts me in a better mood. Pick up a guitar and strum for a while. Draw some squiggles on a sheet of paper. Write a haiku. Doing creative activities can help push those sad thoughts away.

Measure Success by Setting Goals

RECENTLY I WAS CLEANING OUT MY WORK BAG AND I FOUND A CRUM-
pled sheet of paper. On it, I had listed some goals for the previous
year. I made the list during a local writers' group meeting, when a
"success coach" came in to tell us that setting goals is how you get
things done.

I rolled my eyes so hard during her presentation, thinking everything was bullshit. I went through her steps, telling myself, "This
is so dumb." I put it in my bag and forgot about it. When I discovered it almost a year later, I freaked out. I had accomplished almost
everything I'd put on the list. Here are a few:

- I will weigh 240 pounds by October 3, my birthday (holy shit,
  I did this)
- I will start a Web video show by May 5 (I did not do this, but I
  did attempt a podcast, start some new live shows, and, overall, created more cool Internet stuff)
- I will pitch *McSweeney's*, an awesome comedy and culture
  website, ten pieces by July 4 (I sent in about six and had every
  single one rejected, which is fine!)

And I hadn't even considered my goals since I wrote them down.
That's the power of setting goals, the power of your brain to work
behind the scenes and push you toward what you want to get done.

What I learned was, in order to push myself closer to what I
want to become, I need to decide what my goals are. Otherwise, how
can I know if I'm achieving my idea of success?

Before we start writing our goals, we need to figure out what they are.

BEFORE GOALS, PRIORITIES

On a sheet of paper, write down three broad priorities. These aren't goals; they're the higher-level thinking that leads to your goals. They're the unquantifiable things you can't necessarily achieve, but you *can* work toward.

Here's my example: For me, 2015 was about physical and mental fitness, so that was my biggest priority. Then I wanted to express myself creatively, and lastly, help others succeed. So I wrote down:

- Get my mind healthier
- Express myself more
- Help others succeed

These priorities are what you use to come up with your specific goals.

WHO'S ON YOUR SUCCESS TEAM?

You're never alone, even if it feels that way. When you're trying to set and achieve goals, you have folks around who are usually willing to help you. They're part of your success team.

They can be your parents, a coach, a teacher, a friend, a professional mentor, someone from your church, your favorite bartender. Just someone who you know you can go to on occasion and check in with, folks who can be a generally positive influence in your life. Write their names under your priorities. For me, my success team includes a former coworker and an ex-girlfriend I'm still close to.

You're not necessarily going to tell them your goals. This is just a reminder that you have people in your corner who want you to succeed.

WHO'S YOUR ACCOUNTABILITY PARTNER?

Think of one person in your life you can go to about anything. This is going to be your accountability partner. This is a person who you can—but don't necessarily have to—tell your eventual goals to.

Mine is my friend Emily. I've known her for years. She doesn't know she's my accountability partner (she does now!), which is okay. But we both ask each other for advice regularly, we're always telling one another about our longer-term goals, and we are always checking in to see how those plans are going. It developed naturally, so that's why she's mine.

Think of this person as someone to bounce ideas off of later, when you're trying to achieve your goals. See if you can convince him or her to do these exercises with you. Because having another person going through what you're going through is more incentive for *you* to get these goals done.

Why? Because then you become accountable not just to yourself, but to another person. And together, you both have a better chance of succeeding.

Other than that, you don't need to tell your goals to anyone else. The smaller the group who knows your plan, the more likely you are to actually get things done, instead of merely talking about them.

1. Goals must be personal

You want to achieve your own goals, not someone else's. So whatever you write down, it needs to be about you. "I will get Mom to lose ten pounds" isn't a personal goal. But "I will lose ten pounds" is definitely a personal goal.

2. Goals must be positive

Goals are not meant to beat you up. So write them in a way that predicts achievement. Start your statements with this simple phrase: "I will." You're already setting yourself up for success by internalizing whatever you're going to do with the words "I will." You're also making yourself present in the goal, making it personal, and telling yourself it's *going* to happen.

Don't low-key beat yourself up by saying something like "I will stop being so fat." Say "I will lose ten pounds" or "I will start exercising."

3. Goals need a date

Lastly, you need to give your goal a date within the next year. Without a date to achieve a goal, many folks push it off until the future because they don't have a deadline. When you say you will do something by a certain time, your brain's more likely to do it. Each of your goals needs to look like this:

I will [do such-and-such] by [this date].

Some examples:

- I will run a 5K by May 1
- I will finish the first draft of my novel by November 15
- I will ask for a raise by August 10

The dates are somewhat arbitrary. You want them to be realistic, sure, but what's more important is setting the idea of a finish line for your goal. Because then you'll have something to push toward.

4. Write down your three big priorities

Like I said earlier, you need your larger-picture priorities before you can figure out how your goals work to meet them. Here are some broad examples:

- Get healthier in my body
- Finish a large creative project
- Have more financial stability

5. Write down ten goals

It's time to develop your goals. Start by writing ten of them in the above format: staying positive, making them quantifiable, and giving them a date. They don't need to be in any specific order, but after you write each, leave some room on the paper, because we're going to do a bit more.

Look at your goals after you've written them down. See any that you don't think meet your three priorities? That's okay. But you do want to focus on those priorities above everything else. Make sure each priority has at least two goals connected to it.

6. Name three actions per goal

Now that you have your goals, it's time to write down how you're going to achieve them. For each goal, you want to write three actions that are in your control. By that, I mean if your goal is "I will lose ten pounds by May 15," you could write these three actions:

- Walk thirty minutes a day
- Lift weights at the gym three days a week
- Bring my lunch to work every day

These actions are all something you can control. You can track how much you walk using an app for your phone or a pedometer, so you can do that. You may have to change your schedule around, but you can definitely go to the gym three days a week. And it will take some preparation, but you can start bringing your lunch to work each day instead of eating out.

All these actions lead to the eventual goal of losing ten pounds by May 15. So, when you write your actions, make sure they go directly toward your stated goal. You can write more actions, but three is a good amount to start with.

I WROTE MY GOALS — NOW WHAT?

After you've got your goals and your three actions for each, you need to visualize yourself achieving each goal. (This is some hokey shit I always thought was dumb. But, ugh, it *works*. Before I speak in front of a crowd, I always visualize how the opening will go—usually a joke—and the audience exploding in laughter. When I do that, I almost always do a better job. When I don't do it, I have way less confidence, and the audience response isn't as great.) When you internalize your goals by seeing them in your mind, it's like telling your subconscious, "This is important, so do it."

You will soon discover you are pushing yourself toward your goals without thinking about it. Ten goals are a lot to remember, as are the three steps toward each. But when you visualize it, your brain will start moving you in the direction of each goal.

REWRITE YOUR GOALS EVERY DAY OR WEEK

Similar to visualizing, when you rewrite your goals, it's another way of reminding yourself, and your subconscious, that this is what you want to achieve. Every day might be a bit much for some of us, but at least do it weekly. Hammering your goals home fifty-two times this year will definitely make your brain go, "Oh, yeah, maybe we should do this shit!"

LET GO OF THE ATTACHMENT TO RESULTS

Setting goals isn't necessarily about achieving your perfect results. It's more about the journey *toward* your goals. I know that sounds counterproductive, but hear me out: I don't want you to beat yourself up about not achieving all your goals.

Instead, I want you to realize you've made progress, even slow progress, which is better than having achieved no progress. That's where you were before you had any goals. And that's a great thing. No one achieves everything they want to do with their lives overnight. It's all about incremental success.

MAKE MONTHLY/WEEKLY/DAILY GOALS

I get a lot of shit done because I'm always writing lists. You don't need to follow all the steps above on your shorter-term goals, but it's always best to write down everything you need to get done. Because this internalizes it in your brain, and it's a great way to stay on track for the day.

Here's an example of a list I would make for myself (and some of these daily goals go toward my yearly goals, too):

- Go to gym in the morning
- Walk thirty minutes in the morning
- Send e-mail updating team on work project
- Check in with boss on project
- Walk thirty minutes after work
- Call sister to plan her upcoming visit
- Pay mortgage
- Write 1,500 words on novel

Notice how each goal is something I can check off of a list? You get some satisfaction by checking things off. It feels good. But, most importantly, when you write down what you need to get done for the day (or week, or month), it lets you know how to direct your brain.

When I don't write daily lists for myself, I can spend hours on Reddit or Facebook, looking at pointless things that don't help me get my work done. But when I have a list of work to do, well, I get it done.

Here's a nice way to get started: Write down your list of goals, but make the first thing something you've already done for the day, so your list starts off with a success. Now you're already crushing this list! Hell yeah.

REVIEW YOUR GOALS, AND UPDATE THEM ACCORDINGLY

Occasionally you should review your goals, if you're not already regularly rewriting them as suggested above. Visualize yourself finishing each goal. Then look over your three actions, and see if they're not pushing you toward your goal. It's okay to make edits. But don't change your goals because they're harder than you thought they'd be.

It's also okay to decide whether or not a goal is still something you want. If your goal is to learn how to bake, then you realize, "holy shit, baking sucks" (I'm coming for you, Rachael Ray!), you don't need to have that as a goal anymore. The main point of your goals should be to enrich your life and make it better. If it's just making things worse, it's okay to cut your losses and try something new.

Part of the review process is also to see how much you've already accomplished. It's good to occasionally sit back and realize you're moving closer to what you want. That will help keep you on track, which makes you more likely to succeed.

BREAK YOUR GOALS INTO SMALLER CHUNKS

If your goal is "I will lose thirty pounds by July 15," that can be too much to visualize, so even if you lose seven pounds, it may still feel like thirty is almost unachievable. "I will lose five pounds by February 15"—a smaller goal, and a closer date—is easier to visualize, and thus easier to attain.

Last year, one of my goals was to buy a condo. That's a pretty huge goal, which required dozens of steps beforehand. So I broke my larger goal, "I will buy a condo by August 15," down into smaller chunks:

- I will get preapproval for a loan from a mortgage broker by April 30
- I will figure out what neighborhoods I want to live in by May 10
- I will find a real estate agent by May 15
- I will begin looking at homes by May 20

Buying a home is almost something out of my control—maybe the market sucks; maybe there's nothing in my price range I like; maybe my credit sucks (attention, Mom and Dad: it doesn't)—but those other steps definitely aren't.

Break your larger goals into tinier ones and achieve them incrementally. It's much easier to hit those smaller goals.

EVEN IF YOU NEVER LOOK AT YOUR GOALS AGAIN, YOU'RE MORE LIKELY TO ACHIEVE THEM

Our brains are crazy things. So you know how I told you I wrote down that list of goals, those actions and everything else, and then threw it in my bag and forgot it? After I found it later that year, I looked over the list. I actually gasped out loud, and my cat gave me a funny look.

Of the ten goals, I had achieved about half of them. Just by writing down my goals, and what I could do to achieve them, I accomplished half of them. The others I hadn't completely done, but I had worked toward finishing every single one without even realizing it.

All that matters is I took these first steps toward achieving my goals. Thousands of miles can be walked in small steps. So take your first one and get going.

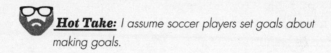 **_Hot Take:_** *I assume soccer players set goals about making goals.*

You Don't Get to Tell Anyone Anything about Their Body

PEOPLE OF ALL SHAPES, SIZES, AND GENDERS CAN DRESS HOWEVER they want, whenever they want, for whatever reason they want. Under no circumstances are we allowed to shame someone for their choices or sexualize their bodies.

Their choices don't affect your life at all.

Has someone dressed in a manner you find tasteless? Who gives a shit. Keep it to yourself.

Perhaps you think someone looks supersexy. Who gives a shit? Keep it to yourself.

This also goes for a person's choices about what to do with his or her body. Do you think tattoos are disgusting? Or piercings? Or muttonchops or green hair or anything else? Simple: Don't do that! Someone else's choice *doesn't affect you at all*.

If someone asks your opinion, give it. If you want to compliment a close friend, you can. If your significant other looks great in jorts, you can tell them. Otherwise, make like a librarian and *shhhhh*.

Whatever Someone Says They Are, That's What They Are

WE DON'T GET TO DECIDE WHETHER SOMEONE'S A SPECIFIC GENDER. Or if they're gay. (Or if they're "they" or "he" or "she" or anything else.) Or asexual. Or if they're an astronaut. Or a writer. Or a "true" gamer. Or literally anything.

Whatever someone tells you they are, that's what they are. You accept it. You don't tell them they're wrong. Or how you *know* they're actually something else. Or ask, "Are you sure?" Or explain how you know other people who call themselves that, and, wow, they totally don't seem like that.

You accept whatever they say they are because that's what they *are*.

If you're ever confused about someone's gender, ask what pronoun they'd like you to use. Don't assume and call someone "sir" or "ma'am" unless you know. Call a group of people "folks" or "people" instead of "guys." Whenever you have a doubt, ask and go with what they say.

The terminology around gender and sexuality and identity is always in flux, too. Accept that. Never be mad because you have to learn something new in order to be respectful and kind toward others. If you're ever confused, ask someone. It's best to err on the side of caution rather than risk making someone feel awful just for existing as they are. And I've probably already gotten some things wrong in this section, because, like I said, things are always changing.

Accept whatever someone tells you they are. Because they decide that, not you. (If you disagree, go read The Asshole Test chapter again.)

Hot Take: *I once stayed in a hotel that was hosting a conference for people who believe some humans are secretly robots. Didn't get any weird looks for once.*

WHAT WOULD TOM HANKS DO?

Tom Hanks is known for being the nicest guy in Hollywood. I've listened to dozens of interviews with him over the years. He never, ever talks shit. He's always kind, gives everyone else credit, and is humble as fuck. That's just who he is.

This man was in *The Ladykillers* remake, which is one of the worst movies ever made. Yet if you asked him about it, he'd tell you how it was a great experience and he learned a lot about himself by doing it. And he was fortunate to work with great people. That's a level of amazingness we should all strive for, to never talk smack, to always be promoting everyone else, and to be as positive as possible. Also, I didn't come up with this concept. Scott Dikkers, one of *The Onion* founders, mentioned it in a class I took with him. (And giving Scott props is exactly what Tom Hanks would do.)

So if you're ever wondering how to deal with a problem in your life, ask yourself, "What Would Tom Hanks Do?" He'd probably be as nice as possible, stay positive and upbeat, and compliment everyone else around him while minimizing his own contributions.

Do that. It'll work.

Jealousy Is Bad!

I'M FORTUNATE TO HAVE MANY FRIENDS WHO ARE HELLA SUCCESS-ful. Some are amazing journalists. Some have jobs on bomb-ass television shows. Some have adorable spouses and created awesome little versions of themselves. (These are sometimes called "babies.") But for a long time, when I saw these people and their success, I would get shitty.

"They don't deserve it," I would tell myself. Then I would think of all the ways I was more deserving. I had worked harder. My work was better than theirs. They were mean and didn't deserve anything. I remember thinking similar thoughts about someone I went to college with *who is a supermodel.* Like, she's on the covers of magazines and I regularly see her face on women's clothing store windows. But when I first saw her success, my brain went, "Psh, that's bullshit. If I worked hard I could also be on the cover of a magazine."

But I didn't and they did. My brain still wanted me to push them down—make them seem shittier and propel myself up. This benefited no one, especially when sometimes I would let my shitty comments out into the real world. I would message a friend with something like, "Ugh, did you see [mutual friend] got that job? What horseshit." (Also, uh, not all of us have the physical, financial, or mental abilities to get some of these things. I mean, hey, Calvin Klein, I'll gladly appear shirtless in an ad if you want me. But I also understand if you politely say no, on account of my body having hair.)

How does this help anyone? It's just electronic proof that I'm a jealous and spiteful dick. Me bitching about someone else's success doesn't make me more successful. Nor does it somehow *stop* that person's success. Not that I should ever want to stop anyone from being successful.

The real problem with jealousy is—and, boy, this will sound familiar—insecurity. I'm feeling attacked by someone else getting something. It's so stupid to think about in retrospect. I still get this way, too, so it's not like I've completely cured myself of it. But what I do know now is a way to fix it.

YOU'RE ONLY COMPETING WITH YOURSELF

Instead of comparing myself with someone else, instead I judge myself against me from six months ago. That's much more objective. How the hell do I expect to compare myself with a supermodel I went to college with? Impossible. But Andy Boyle from a while ago? I can compare myself with that dude. All I'm trying to do is make sure I'm progressing forward, that I'm getting better at things, that I'm taking stock and seeing how I'm doing.

So whenever that bullshit jealousy monster rears its ugly green head, I just look back on my life. I think, "Six months ago I was here. Now I'm here. I am doing better. That is awesome. Hell yeah, me." And then I mentally and physically high-five myself and go on with my day. (High-fiving yourself in public is a fun way to make people give you sideways glances.)

Jealousy is normal. Acting shitty because of it is behavior you can fix. So compare yourself only with yourself. Be happy you know successful people. Competition is good. Jealousy is not.

Compare yourself only with yourself.

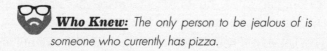

Who Knew: *The only person to be jealous of is someone who currently has pizza.*

Flipping from Negative to Positive

FLIPPING THINGS FROM NEGATIVE TO POSITIVE IN YOUR HEAD IS A great way to retrain your brain. You can do it with almost anything. Instead of viewing something as shitty, try to see the positive behind it. Here are some simple exercises to help you with that.

■ **What's pissing you off right now?** Think about what's the biggest problem in your life. Try to break it down to its smallest bits. Is it actually a real problem? Or is it something you're *making* into a problem? If it's a problem, that means it can be solved. So either you should work toward actually solving it or you should stop viewing it as a problem.

> *If it's a problem, that means it can be solved.*

Maybe the biggest problem in your life is your boss. Your life has three constants: death, taxes, and shitty bosses. Perhaps they're constantly changing their minds about their priorities, so you can never get your work done. Or they blame you for their own managerial problems. Or perhaps they take you into the break room, tell you to leave the door open, and then scream at you about how you suck at your job until you almost cry. (*No way is this a personal anecdote* [yes, it is].)

But here's the thing about shitty bosses: After you work for them, you quickly understand a few things. The first is if you're ever in a boss position, you know how *not* to treat people underneath you. The second is you can quickly see these terrible behaviors everywhere, so you learn to avoid them in others. Third, whenever you're interviewing for a future job, you can see the asshole tendencies in anyone who may employ you.

While working for them might suck right now, it's going to help you out so much in the future. (You may even have the opportunity someday to write a book that proves that one boss wrong who said you would never amount to anything, too!) Boom. Flipped this negative thing to positive.

■ **Review the situation.** It's easy to think someone or something is against you. Someone screws up your order at a restaurant. Or a coworker does something wrong on a project after you told her to do it otherwise. You can view these incidents as proof the world is against you. Or you can realize maybe you're not viewing the situation correctly.

Someone supersmart once said, "Never attribute to malice what you can attribute to ignorance." (Probably Neil deGrasse Tyson. He's so smart!) Sometimes we feel like the world is against us, when actually, people make mistakes.

The woman at Starbucks who used soy instead of whole milk didn't do it because she hates you. She's had a busy day and makes a hundred drinks an hour, so she's allowed to make a few mistakes. Your coworker is doing her best, probably with other deadlines you're not aware of, and odds are you didn't communicate exactly what you wanted as clearly as possible. No one's perfect, so don't expect absolute perfection always.

■ **How could this be your fault instead?** Many times I want to lash out at someone else before I actually realize the problem wasn't them: It was me. This is pretty common for most people.

You want a problem solved, and it's easier to attack someone else than to look within for the solution. If I just take a second and think things through, I usually find out I can solve the problem myself and it's not actually someone else's fault.

■ **Instead of being mad, what else can you be?** When your in-stinct is to go negative, realize you're doing that and stop and think about why. Are you mad at a person? A place? A situation?

Okay, now that you've realized what's causing you to feel this way, what is it *about* the person/place/situation that's making you feel that way? You want to drill down to the action or thing that's actually causing you to feel angry. Then think it through even more: Is this an action someone is in control of? If not, then are you really justified in being angry?

If they are in control of the action, are they *aware* they're doing something that's making you mad? If not, then they aren't acting with malice, so maybe your anger is misplaced. Always think through what else you can feel instead of anger at a situation, and odds are you'll find a less negative emotion.

■ **Find the sunny side.** That dumb phrase about there being a sil-ver lining behind every dark rain cloud never made sense to me. Instead, I think it's better to know that behind every dark rain cloud is the goddamn sun. Even if you think there's no good thing to ever come out of a situation, it doesn't mean there won't ever be good things again. The sun will continue to shine.

For some people, one of the shittiest things that can happen is breaking up with someone. It feels like nothing will ever be good again. But it's better to break up now instead of in ten years from now when you have three children and despise one another.

So even though a situation could be shitty, there's always going to be something positive that comes from it. Maybe it isn't totally obvious now. Look for it.

■ ■ ■

When bad shit happens, think about anything positive that can come from it and focus on that. Your car got hit by a drunk driver while you were asleep. Well, the positive is you could've been in the car when it happened, but you weren't. Or the positive could be the drunk driver could've run off the road, and instead he's safe.

Still, overall, shitty things happen, but when you're trying to focus on the positive aspect of a situation, it can help overshadow how shitty it is.

Whenever possible I try to find at least three positive things about an awful situation. They usually fall under a few categories:

- Things could've been worse.
- I learned from this.
- I still have my health.

And in the end, most bad shit falls under this last category: This will someday make an interesting story to share with others and make them laugh. Or perhaps it'll become an anecdote for an amazing advice book someone will someday read. *Like this one!* Huzzah, we've come full circle.

Pro Tip: *Flipping from negative to positive is always a good idea, unless you're trying to jump start your car.*

In Conclusion,
Mostly Good Rules to Live By

1. Don't be an asshole.
2. Just because you were an asshole, it doesn't mean you still have to be.
3. You can always change for the better.
4. Success comes when you put others before yourself.
5. You will always suck before you get better.
6. You're competing only against yourself.
7. Present yourself positively so people will judge you accordingly.
8. Read more.
9. Mental and physical health are important, so spend time on them.
10. Never ask anyone if she's pregnant. Just don't.

SOCIAL
Awesomeness

You Don't Have to
Stay Friends with Everyone

IMAGINE YOU OWN A STOVE. NOW, THIS STOVE HAS BEEN IN YOUR
life ten years. When you first began cooking with it, the appliance
worked great. You made lots of cakes and cookies and tasty pizza
inside of it. But after years and years of use, the stove changed.
(And so have you.) Now it randomly shoots out acrid smoke, even
when you're not using it. The food you make in it always ends up
smelling like a wet dog, and wet-dog pizza is gross.

Even though that stove served you well for those first few years,
is it worth keeping the stove around, now that it's not acting the
same way? I would say it's time to get a new stove. Sure, you may
have to rely on the microwave more for a while. Or maybe get take-
out. But if your stove is acting terrible, you should make a change.

Same goes with friends. Now, you'll probably call me callous
and say people aren't as disposable as appliances. They're not, obviously. But so often I hear from my friends about the awful people in
their lives. So I tell them, "Why don't you just stop being friends
with that person?" And the main excuse I hear is, "But we've been
friends forever!" So? "But we have so much shared history!" And?
"But they just *get* me!" Yeah, but it sounds like they're shitty as hell
and making your life overall worse.

This sounds harsh. Partially because we're raised wrong and
act as if friendships never change or go away. Just like romantic relationships change shape or end, so can friendships. But *unlike* romantic relationships, I think you end a friendship a little differently.

Ghosting is a time-honored tradition in dating where you go
out with someone a few times and then disappear, never to be
heard from again. You just stop texting the person or responding

to his or her social media messages. You vanish. This makes a person feel shitty, and you shouldn't do it with someone you've smooched.

But with friends? Totally acceptable. Because if they're your friends, when you ghost them it's just you signaling to them your relationship is changing. In a romantic setting, when you ghost someone, it's shitty and mean, because it indicates you're *done* with another human being without giving them the courtesy of a conversation. Whereas in a friendship, you have lots of friendship history. You're just moving to a new stage of your friendship.

I call this going from friends to acquaintances. Whenever someone who you've realized is a shitty part of your life asks to hang out, you're always busy. If they wanna talk, you don't respond fast because, again, you're busy. You just keep doing this until they get the hint and move on. If you instead had a conversation that was, like, "Hey, you're a shitty friend, and you need to change or I'm out," well, that's a great way to make an enemy.

Because the sad truth is, most people won't change. Friends won't. People you date won't. Even though this book is all about changing yourself for the better, unless they're actively reading this book (and you should in fact buy ten copies for each friend you know) or trying to improve their life in other ways, they probably won't listen to you. I've had many conversations like this—on the receiving end, too—and nobody usually changes. (Same thing goes if you tell someone you need some time to yourself. If they're truly toxic in your life, they'll probably be toxic when you try to end things, too.)

So now you've got someone pissed at you. Whereas if you stop being a close friend with someone and become an acquaintance, you can still be kind to them. If you run into them at a party, it's not going to be *as* awkward as if you had told them, "You suck and I don't like you anymore." Also, you can help acquaintances. It just means they're not as big a part of your life.

Think about your closest friends. How many are making your life better? How many are awful? Cultivate the former and think about whether or not you should distance yourself from the latter. As I've aged (read: gotten more bald), the more I've realized this to be true: The people you surround yourself with influence your personality more than anything else. If you're sad all the time, well, are you surrounding yourself with garbage people?

When I stopped drinking, a lot of my friends disappeared. I think most left because I realized the only thing we had in common was that we got tanked together, so I stopped hanging out. I don't even think it was a conscious decision. I just stopped doing the same things many of them did. So they stopped asking me to get together. (I'm sure the same thing happens if you became friends with people because you climb mountains together and do nothing else except talk mountain climbing and then you suddenly decide, fuck it, I'm a kayaker, no more mountains. Your mountain friends will probably disappear, which is understandable, because mountains are *hard* to kayak.) My life is still awesome, even if my friend group has changed. Your social circle is always changing and evolving, just like you should be.

> **_Pro Tip:_** The only real reason to stay friends with a truly terrible person is if they own a boat. I'm kidding, of course—it should be a really big boat.

Making Friends

I'VE BEEN LUCKY ENOUGH TO WORK IN A BUNCH OF DIFFERENT CIT-
ies. From internships to full-time jobs, I've hopped around the
United States a bunch, like a traveling circus with way less animal
cruelty. And in each city, I had to start over when it came to friends.
So I quickly learned how to make some, because buddies make life
more exciting.

> **Friendship note:** You don't *have* to have tons of friends.
> Being a loner, or having just a few good friends, is to-
> tally fine. But I think having more people in your life
> helps you out. It gives you people to talk to, people to go
> on adventures with, people you can learn from. All of
> those enrich your life. I'm typing this chapter while sit-
> ting across from my good friend Mel, who just wanted
> to hang out and write together. Nifty!

100 PERCENT PERFECT AND NOT AT ALL BULLSHIT WAYS TO MAKE FRIENDS

1. Get to know people at work

You've got a decent chance of meeting people at your job who you'll
want to hang out with outside of work. If your job has younger people,
folks are already getting together after work. So ask to join them.

2. Join clubs

Have you ever wanted to learn how to ballroom dance? Are you
bad at bowling but want to get better? Sick of playing chess with

(and losing to) your cat? No matter the city you live in, odds are, groups of people are getting together and doing things they dig. All you need to do is find when those groups meet and show up (check online for shit in your town). You'll be getting together with people who have a shared interest—you'll already have something in common to talk about!

> **Friendship note:** Most of your friendship-making success involves just showing up and talking to people. (Just like most success in life!) Whenever you're somewhere, just start talking to strangers, as long as they don't seem too crazypants.

3. Take a class

Every decent-sized city has places that offer classes, from cooking to writing to improv comedy to playing chess. (That cat's going DOWN.) Find a few that seem interesting (and within your budget), and sign up. When you're taking a class, just like when you join a club, half the work is done for you, because you're meeting people with a similar interest. So you already have something to talk about and you have something to relate to. Friendship magic! (Also, take a magic class. Even the hardest cynic loves magic.)

> **Friendship note:** You do not have to be awesome at something to take a class in it. That's why you're taking a class. Never feel bad about your skill level! You're there to learn and get better and make friends. Don't worry about becoming the Next Great Thing.

4. Talk to strangers at bars

When I was younger, I made a lot of friends at bars. Because, like I keep pointing out, we had something in common: We liked to drink and sit. So we could start chatting about that right off! Huzzah. I know it was easier for me to do this because I'm a man (this is me checking my privilege), so social interactions at bars were generally less about, uh, going to make-out town than it may be for women (generally). I used to go to bars with a book and just start reading. Sure enough, someone would want to talk to me about my book, and suddenly I'd made a new pal. One who could read!

5. Volunteer

Not only is volunteering awesome, but it's a great way to meet like-minded folks with similar interests. There's that thing again: putting yourself in situations with people who are like you. It's almost as if that's a theme of this chapter about making friends! Research places you can volunteer at near you and then start showing up. If you like the people you volunteer with, ask them if they'd like to get together sometime. If they're the kinds of people who regularly volunteer, they're probably the kinds of cool humans you want in your life anyway.

6. Search on Meetup.com for random things

It's a nifty website, and most cities have a lot of different groups on there. Search for a few that interest you, then start showing up and talking to people. Just watch out: Sometimes the groups are started for scammy promotional purposes. But if it's a group of people who get together and talk about nineteenth-century literature, you probably don't have to worry about that.

7. Use dating apps

On most of them you can set that you're looking for "just friends." Sure, people don't always follow that. But I've made some good pals through dating websites who just wanted friendship. And through them, I made even more friends. So it all worked out.

■ ■ ■

The main way you make friends is by going where like-minded people are, being pleasant, and contributing something to the conversation. Put out your hand, introduce yourself to strangers, and ask them about the thing you are probably both interested in.

Be open, be helpful, and be kind, and you'll make friends. I promise.

HELPFUL NOTE: *Some of my friends I haven't seen in person in years and we stay besties by talking online a lot. Some of my friends I've made through the Internet and I've never met them in person. If either works for you, that's great, as long as you feel good about those relationships. My friend Emily once went to a wedding where part of the wedding party was the groom's World of Warcraft guild, who he met in person for the first time that weekend. Isn't that awesome? Wherever you can find them, just make sure your friends are people who make you feel good about being you.*

Pro Tip: Even if you're a terrible person, the easiest way to make friends is to own a really big boat.

Be Good to Whoever Raised You

MOST OF MY LATE TWENTIES WAS SPENT TRYING TO MAKE UP FOR how much of a little shit I was to my parents in the previous few decades. I was quite the handful in high school (aren't we all?), and in college I wasn't any better. I was mean to my mom, especially. Just a total jerk. Which is why part of being an adult is realizing you should always be a good kid to your parents. (And thus should dedicate your first book to them.)

I know not everyone's parents are great. Some of you were raised by grandparents, or maybe an aunt or uncle, or in some other situation. But if you were fortunate enough to have someone around who raised you, and you have some sort of positive relationship with them, you should be good to them. They raised you, even if they did a shitty job. Most people don't *want* to do a shitty job of raising kids. It's just hard as hell.

My mom always said she and my dad knew they were going to mess up me and my sister juuuuuust a little bit, but they tried their best not to mess us up big-time. That's what most good parents do: try their best. So try your best to be good back.

1. Call them sometimes

Give them a ring every few days. They raised you for a reason: because they like you. Or were required by law. Either way, they have a vested interest in knowing how you're doing. So give them a call every once in a while. I call my mom most Sundays while I take a long walk. I give my pops a call every few weeks.

My mom generally keeps me up-to-date on my dad's comings and goings. ("You will *not* believe what *your father* did this time."

Whenever one of your parents refers to the other as "your father" or "your mother," someone's in trouble. DO NOT PICK SIDES. It will end disastrously.) Even if you're friends with your parents on Facebook and Instagram and Snapchat and Friendster (lol), nothing beats a phone call. (For those of you younger than me, the Friendster thing is a joke. It was like Facebook before Facebook, except it sucked.)

2. Go see them

You must see them face-to-face on occasion. When I lived in Florida, thousands of miles away from my family, I could go see them only twice a year, if I was lucky. That definitely wasn't enough for them. Now that I'm older and can afford to travel, I head home more regularly.

I want to be a part of their lives. And they definitely want me to be a part of theirs. Being around your parents won't kill you. It'll make you a better person, even if your parents are annoying. (All parents are slightly annoying. It's their job.)

3. Steal their brainpower

For many of us, our parents also lived through a lot of shit. That means they know a lot. This is called "wisdom" and you should tap into it.

When I decided to buy a home, I called my parents and got their advice. When I was negotiating for a new job, I called them and asked their advice. When I was trying to figure out what was wrong with my toilet, I called my dad. (Once before, I had called my mom for toilet advice. After she took a long pause, she informed me that toilet questions were better suited for my father.) They've lived through most of the same dumb things you're going to experience. So smarten yourself up by listening to them.

OTHER WAYS TO BE GOOD TO YOUR PARENTS

- Buy your mom flowers on Mother's Day.
- Get your dad comfortable socks (dads *love* comfy socks).
- Don't be a little shit and hate the Yankees just because your mom *loves* the Yankees. (Other reasons for hating the Yankees? Just fine.)
- When they call, answer your goddamn phone. You can take ten minutes out of your day to talk to the people who spent probably hundreds of thousands of dollars on your life.
- Understand they probably won't have the exact same political views as you, and that's okay, so you don't need to be a complete jerk to them about it.
- Let them know when they use a word that's considered racist or otherwise hurtful, even if it *is* a word they used growing up.
- They've got feelings and get sad, so be there for them, even if they weren't flawlessly 100 percent there for you.
- When your dad gets into cherry red Corvettes in his sixties, make sure you let him know how cool cherry red Corvettes are, even if you don't know a goddamn thing about cherry red Corvettes.
- Console your retired mother when your retired father buys *a second cherry red Corvette, and then claims he bought it on ACCIDENT.* ON ACCIDENT!
- If they want to visit you, say yes, because they want to see your life and your world. They get superexcited about those visits.
- When they visit you, if your mom thinks your furniture arrangement sucks, she's probably right, so hear her out.

- When visiting them, eat the thing your mom or dad always loved making you when you were little, because it makes them happy.

- Let your mom tease you on social media.

- Tell them "I love you" whenever you have the chance, because you never know when you may not have the chance. I know it's corny, but hey, life sometimes is. That's why we still buy Hallmark cards.

Hot Take: Be good to whoever raised you, especially if you were raised by wolves. They're not fully domesticated, you know.

Don't Ruin Your Life
on Social Media

ONE STATUS UPDATE CAN RUIN YOUR LIFE. THAT'S THE POWER SOCIAL media has these days. So you should use it wisely. Thankfully, I'm okay at it, so here's how to not suck.

1. If you hesitate, don't post it

Whenever I stop to think about whether or not I should be putting something up on one of my feeds, that's usually a great indicator it's a bad idea. Why else would my brain be going, "Whoa, dude, let's think this one through!" unless there's an issue? Nine times out of ten, my instincts are right, so I don't post whatever caused me to pause.

2. Post knowing your mom and boss can read it

My mom and my boss follow me on Twitter. One of them is forced to love me; the other decides whether I get a paycheck. I want them both happy. I always consider what they're going to think when I put something out in the world. If I think it might offend them, it's not something I want out there.

3. Don't talk shit

Pissed at your boss? Think a client is an idiot? Want to tell off a coworker? Complain to your mom, not to the world. Publicly talking shit is the dumbest thing you can do. Don't do it.

4. Don't vaguebook

This is where you write something like, "Wow, have a problem much? Some people just don't know when to keep their mouths shut. But don't worry. I know. I'm listening. I'm aware. And I'm coming for you." This is the writing of a person who's gone nutso. Whenever someone writes something like this, I assume they got in a shouting match with their dog because it wouldn't stand still for an Instagram photo.

Or when someone writes, "I'm so happy, but I can't tell any of you yet! OMG, this is great!!!" We get it: You want us to know you're leading such a fantastic life that's so full of amazing, but you also want to include an air of mystery to make it seem even more fantastic, when you probably just got a 20 percent off coupon in the mail for Bed Bath & Beyond. But vaguebooking sounds cooler than bragging about saving three dollars on a new plunger. Please stop.

5. Don't publicly bash a former significant other

This is an extension of not talking shit. It happens so regularly, it deserves its own section (see "The Asshole Test"). Nothing good comes from being publicly mean about someone you used to care about. Nothing. Instead, write some angry songs or terrible poetry on your Tumblr.

6. Don't punch down

Making jokes on social media is awesome. Making jokes at the expense of an already marginalized group is not awesome. It's what an asshole does. Making fun of an entire group of people who society already regularly beats up is just piling on. It makes you look bad. Instead, if you have to punch, punch up: Make fun of groups with mountains of privilege. Great topics include Congress, celebrities who are famous only because they are famous, and Bono.

7. Don't post a person's photo without his or her permission

The main reason people post photos of strangers is to make fun of them. Usually it's because the person looks different, or is doing something embarrassing. That's shitty and mean. Think about how you'd feel if someone did that to you. Pretty icky, right? So if you're going to post anything about another person, ask permission first. Because you *should* post a photo of someone because what they're doing is *awesome*. Otherwise, you're a shithead. Don't be a shithead.

8. Don't argue politics

In the history of the Internet, no one's mind has ever been changed because of an argument on social media. Never. Not once. Especially no one's uncle. Now, faced with that fact, you think you're going to be the one to buck the trend? I don't think so.

9. Be positive

The older I get, the less I want to follow humans who are super-negative all the time on social media. Maybe it's because I'm less full of hatred for the world, but also because being happy is rad. So try to help make the Internet more happy by attempting to be positive sometimes.

10. Share other people's stuff

Social media is mostly about being social. If it's the You Show the entire time, even when we've all been told to "build our personal brand," it can get a bit boring. Share cool work your friends—and even strangers!—are doing.

11. It's okay to delete things

Less is always better, especially on social media.

If you share something and have second thoughts about it, just delete it. You probably don't even need to explain you deleted it. Just do it and feel better about yourself. Less is always better, especially on social media.

12. Turn off notifications

Social media is a time suck. Unless your job requires you to be on it constantly (I'm so sorry for you), make it so your phone and computer never receive notifications about updates. You should have to go to Facebook or Twitter or Instagram or whatever to get your updates. Your social media news shouldn't come to you. Otherwise you'll spend the majority of your time responding to every little like or comment. That's not healthy for your brain, or your productivity.

FINAL NOTE: *Never get in a pissing match with a skunk, or with anyone online. Because you both end up smelling like shit, except the skunk doesn't care. (Thanks, Mom, for this great adage.)*

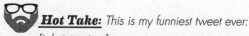 ***Hot Take:*** *This is my funniest tweet ever:*
[job interview]
"You have to pass a drug test."
-No problem.
interviewer pulls out an apple
"Make me a bong in 30 seconds."
-Oh shit.

Put Shit in Your Calendar

AS SOON AS YOU GET ANY SORT OF AN APPOINTMENT, PUT IT IN your electronic calendar, preferably one you can easily access on your phone. If you don't have one, get one.

While you're setting this up, also put in every birthday you need to remember (your mom's, your dad's, your siblings', your weed dealer's). Then add any major holidays or days you get off from work. Then include any other big life deadlines, so you know when you gotta get shit done.

Whenever you make plans with someone, immediately put them in this calendar. You should never be late again. Forgetting about plans makes you a jerk, so don't be one.

> **Who Knew:** The word month came from "moonth," because months were roughly one lunar cycle. The term "week" came from that tired feeling you get after keeping up appearances for seven whole days.

ALWAYS BE GOOD TO PEOPLE IN THE SERVICE INDUSTRY

The people who work in the service industry are saints. They spend most of the day on their feet, dealing with lots of jerks. If you treat them poorly, you're a bad person.

If you ordered a meal at a restaurant and your order came out wrong, don't be a jerkstore. Someone made a mistake. Maybe they misheard you because they had a thousand orders coming at them. Or perhaps you *thought* you ordered one thing, but actually you *forgot* to ask for your burger without pickles. Or maybe the kitchen fucked up.

Either way, a mistake happened. Be kind. They'll fix it 99 percent of the time. Then you give them a decent tip because they fixed it. Don't view them as people who are worthless and suck at life because of this one thing. View them as humans deserving of your respect because they did their damn best to please you.

Maybe you've had a service job at some point. Maybe not. Either way, connect with your inner busboy and don't be a dick.

Dealing with Roommates

MOST OF US HAVE TO DEAL WITH ROOMMATES AT SOME POINT IN our lives. Maybe in your dorm room. Maybe in your first post-graduation apartment. Definitely if you make it onto the cast of *Real World: Toledo*.

You've got a handful of ways to get roommates. Let's look at the pros, cons, and potential nightmares.

MOVING IN WITH A GOOD FRIEND

You're both heading to the Big City, and you were such great pals in college, so it just makes sense to share on rent and live together. What could go wrong? Everything.

Living with another human means you have to be totally cool with sharing everything. This ranges from your pots and pans to time in front of the television in your only living room. Or figuring out who gets to use the bathroom when you both have to be at work by nine a.m. (During one summer internship, I lived with two other interns. I would always try to run to the bathroom first, then text the other roommate from inside the bathroom to let him know I was coming out, so he got second dibs before the roommate we both didn't like. If that third roommate is reading this now, I'm sorry, we were jerks.)

You'll want to have a long talk with your good friend before moving in together about how to compromise and settle griev-ances. If she's supermessy and you're a clean freak, how will you deal with that? Who will take out the trash? Who gets to watch television after work? What if you're a partier and your roommate is studying for med school? You'll need to hash out all these things *before* deciding whether living together is going to be a good idea.

I lived with one person during a summer internship who I'd become good friends with online before we moved in together. I thought it was going to be great. But then we started getting in fights over who could watch the television in the living room. Or who could use the one bathroom for long periods of time while the other *really, really, really* had to pee and ended up going in the backyard. All because we never discussed how we would deal with these conflicts. So eventually we just spent all our time in our rooms, pissed at each other, until we both moved out and then basically never talked again.

This is what happens between you and a good friend if you don't discuss how you're going to communicate about your problems. So have that talk up front. And figure out whether or not this friendship is worth destroying through living together, because that's always a possibility.

FINDING SOMEONE ON CRAIGSLIST OR WHEREVER

This is another big way people end up finding roommates. You move to a new city, they've got a room available, and you meet up with everyone and they seem cool and they like you. The thing is, you don't know what they're *actually* like. Because, just like when you're on a first date, everyone is on their best behavior and trying to seem as chill as possible.

Then you discover your new roommate likes to sit in his underwear on your couch in the living room. And he never bathes. Or he leaves half-empty cups of yogurt on the counter for days and days. You never know what you're getting with Craigslist. But just like moving in with someone you actually know, you need to figure out how you'll resolve issues.

When showing up to a place you may move into, check how

clean it is. Is the trash empty or overflowing? Does the fridge look like someone's committing a crime against nature and science? How many unwashed dishes are in the sink? If they're not tidying up when they're trying to get a new roommate, they sure as shit aren't tidying up normally. So beware.

Ask them what they do for fun. If all they can say is they go to bars and parties and get drunk, then that's what you're living with: people who will probably be too hungover a lot of the time to take care of basic roommate chores. If you're okay with it, that's fine. I lived in a super punk rock house one summer in college, where everyone was too hungover to do anything, with dirty dishes in the sink and used glasses strewn around the house. The place was a mess and it ruled. It was exactly what I needed when I was twenty. (Yup, twenty. I was drinking underage. I'm a bad boy. Take *that*, cops!) But now that I'm older, in comparison, I die inside when friends are over and don't put their used glasses in my sink. These friends are animals, but thankfully, I am here to tame them.

WILL YOU HAVE TO BE ON THE LEASE?

If you're moving in somewhere new and you can stay off the lease, that's always awesome. If it turns out whoever you're living with is nutso or hard to deal with, you can just find a new place and move. It's *much* harder to do when your name is on the lease.

Never, ever move into a place with a roommate and put only your name on the lease. That means you're liable for everything. Your roommate (or roommates) won't have any ownership over breaking shit or handing the rent in on time. That'll all be on you. And no matter what your would-be roommates say, if they're not on the lease, they're not responsible for anything.

Always check your local rules regarding leases. In some cities, they're awesome for renters. In others, they're terrible for you. Most places have some sort of "renters' rights" organization, which exists to help you understand the law. Discover what you could possibly be on the hook for—and what your landlord is required to do—before signing anything.

TIPS FOR ROOMMATE HAPPINESS

1. Don't be so messy that your roommate wants to get you on *Hoarders*.
2. Don't eat your roommate's food.
3. Bathe regularly.
4. Wash your clothes and sheets and towels regularly.
5. Pay everything on time.
6. Buy a good toilet plunger, the kind with the flange on the end.
7. Ask before throwing a party.
8. If you have a significant other who always spends the night, at some point that person should start paying rent.
9. Don't try to sleep with a roommate.

WHAT TO DO IF YOUR ROOMMATE IS A DEMON SPAWNED IN THE DEEPEST, DARKEST PARTS OF HELL, LIKE THE PART WHERE THEY INVENTED THE PHRASE "GUAC IS EXTRA"

Ever since a caveman decided to share his rental cave with another Cro-Magnon, and then he found out the Cro-Magnon always left his mastodon meat on the coffee table, we've been trying to answer this question. Your first step is communication. If your roommate's awful, explain what's bothering you. If he or she is willing to change, awesome. If not, only one solution remains: Find a way to escape.

If you're not on the lease, find a new place to live. If you are, talk to your landlord about the terrible situation. Maybe you can find someone to take over your spot and move into your room. Otherwise, you just have to deal with it. Your lease will eventually end. In the meantime, find hobbies outside of your home.

It's going to suck. But there are worse things than having a terrible roommate. Like racism and cancer, or cancer that causes racism. (That's about it, though.)

FINAL THOUGHTS: *I was lucky enough to stop having roommates by twenty-three. I also was willing to pay extra to no longer have them. At some point, you may hit that level, too. It's totally okay. Having a roommate can suck. But it's also nice to have someone around you can talk to. Overall, just be kind and thoughtful to the person you're living with, and things will probably go pretty dandy. Also, it's way more acceptable to sit on the couch in your underwear if you don't have roommates.*

Pro Tip: *The most perfect roommate splits rent and utilities with you and then lives at his or her significant other's apartment.*

Buying Gifts

THE BASICS FOR BUYING GIFTS ARE SIMPLE.

1. If it's for a person who lets you touch his or her butt, buy an experience instead of a thing, such as tickets to a play or a meal at a nice restaurant or an afternoon skydiving together. (Note to all future girlfriends: Do not buy me tickets to go goddamn skydiving.)

2. If it's for a friend or family member, think about things or subjects they like, then walk around in a mall or go online and pick the first thing you think they'd enjoy. It truly is the thought that counts. (Even if you pick something shitty, they won't tell you because they like you. Success!)

3. If you're stumped for ideas, buy the person a book. Preferably this one.

**Hot Take:** Kids give the worst gifts. "Thanks for the macaroni art, I guess. It's like you didn't even check my Amazon wish list."

When It's Time to Party
We Will Party Hard

PARTIES, LIKE MOST THINGS IN LIFE, ARE MEANT TO BE FUN. THEY can also, like most things in life, turn wildly disastrous. Thankfully, you're reading a book written by a Party Master (I once brought most of my college dorm floor—about fifty people—to a party. I don't fuck around). I'm here to help you party responsibly.

Whether you're partying at work or just hitting up a friend's kegger, abide by this list. Or you're going to have a bad time. IMPORTANT LEGAL NOTE: You should follow all applicable laws regarding drugs and alcohol wherever you live. Just because I did stupid things and drank underage doesn't mean you should. Above all, be safe and responsible.

- **Don't have sex in the bathroom.** People need to poop and pee in there, and if you're doing the ol' potato toss, people can't poop *or* pee. Also, if you really want to have sex that badly, go to your or your partner's home.

- **Don't have sex in general.** Odds are, you and the other person have been drinking. People who are drinking generally can't consent to sexual activities. Therefore, if you're at a party and drinking, you can't have sex because you can't have consent.

- **If you puke, clean it up.** This is pretty self-explanatory.

- **Kick yourself out.** If you find yourself getting aggressive with others, it's time to leave the party. When you get to that level of Party Town where you feel the need to shout at strangers, or feel like you wanna fight someone, get an Uber and go home.

■ **Bring your own booze, plus a little extra.** It's always nice to show up with a twelve-pack of beer, even when you plan on drinking only eleven. That one extra beer can help you make a friend.

■ **Don't drink eleven beers at a party.** In general, parties are a great way to meet people and make new friends, or impress your bosses and coworkers. If you're shithoused, you will do the opposite of impress them.

■ **Hydrate.** For every alcoholic beverage you have, drink a big-ass glass of water. Not only will it keep you hydrated and help out with any potential hangovers, but it'll also slow down your alcohol consumption. Sure, you'll have to pee a lot. But it's a small price to pay toward looking less like an idiot.

■ **Don't be that guy.** In all situations in life, whatever "that guy" is, do not be that.

> *Whatever "that guy" is,*
> *do not be that.*

■ **Don't play volunteer DJ.** You aren't in charge of the music unless the host says you are. So don't bogart the stereo and throw on your own jams. Maybe someone spent hours coming up with the perfect party mix (*yes, I have done this*) and now you're wrecking those expertly crafted vibes. C'mon, be cool.

■ **Play it cool.** If you're interested in someone at the party, don't be creepy about it. (See "Don't Be Creepy" for more on this.)

■ **Just leave already.** You don't have to say good-bye to everyone when you leave. How many times do you remember someone *not* telling you good-bye from a party? *Never.* Just find the people you like or were talking to, tell them you're leaving, then bounce. It's that simple!

- **If you've been drinking at all, don't drive home. Ever.** This is the dumbest shit you can do in your life. Not only can you kill yourself, you can kill others. Get a Lyft home.

- **Be discreet.** Don't be the guy who does cocaine in front of everyone. Do cocaine in the bathroom alone, or with a friend, like eighties movies told me you're supposed to. (But don't do drugs. Obviously.)

- **But it's okay to share.** If you're smoking weed, check if anyone around you wants to partake. That's just good manners. (Unless you're at an office party. Then you shouldn't be smoking weed or doing cocaine. Unless you work at Goldman Sachs...?)

A quick general note about drug use: I think people should do only, at maximum, an Obama amount of drugs. That is, an amount so little that you can write about it in your autobiography and then successfully run for president.

- **Keep it down.** If you're outside the house for any reason, don't be superloud. Volume is why the police get called. The cops are one of the main reasons parties end. Also, sometimes cops arrest people at a party. So, don't be noisy outside, and save the party.

- **Stay cool.** If the police show up, be cool and calm and don't say a goddamn word. Usually cops just want you to be quieter and they don't want to write fifty tickets for all the slightly illegal bullshit most of you are doing. So if you're cool, they'll be cool. So be cool, honey bunny, be cool.

- **Chip in.** When the eventual beer run happens later in the night, pony up a few bucks to help out, even if you don't plan on drinking. It's just the kind thing you should do as the guest of a party. Bringing snacks never hurts, either.

- **Don't steal shit.** C'mon. Don't be that asshole.

- **Get the hint.** If the party is dying and it's just you and the host and a handful of people, it's probably time to bounce. Especially if it's obvious the host wants people to leave so he, or she, can hook up with that cute person he's been hanging out with. Don't be a creep; just leave and let them do their thang.

> **Pro Tip:** *The only good reason to have condomless sex is on purpose.*

Advice from a Guy Who No Longer Drinks

1. **Never do shots.** They only lead to you making terrible decisions. Like doing more shots and then puking out the window of a moving car.

2. **IPAs are garbage.** I don't care what anyone says. They are stupid and overpriced and dumb. Drink literally anything else. If I may make a suggestion, Miller High Life is the champagne of beers for a reason. (Because it's delicious and you should drink it for celebrations.)

3. **Drinking a craft beer doesn't make you better than someone drinking a Pabst Blue Ribbon.** Get over yourself. Just because you paid nine dollars for a beer doesn't mean that beer is somehow better. It means you got swindled out of more money for something featuring a different name.

4. **Always eat food before you drink.** Preferably something with lots of fats and carbs. It'll help you soak up the terrible decisions you're about to make.

5. **If you've spent a night drinking, you don't need to eat pizza at two a.m., despite what your dumb friends think.** (FYI: Your dumb friend in many situations is just your subconscious.)

6. **Go to the bar and parties to drink, not to make out.** A person who has been drinking can't consent to anything romantic. Doing things with people who can't consent is illegal. You may be saying, "But what if they've had just a few drinks?" How do *you* know how much they've actually had to drink?

How do *you* know they're actually in the right state of mind to consent to anything? You don't. So don't.

7. **If you have even a single drink, don't drive.** You don't know how strong that beverage is. You don't know if your body will decide to metabolize it differently today, making you unable to operate a motor vehicle safely. Your judgment is always impaired no matter how many drinks you've had. So are you really the best judge of your ability to move a vehicle that can not only kill you, but kill other people? Nope. Get home some other way.

8. **No good texts have ever been sent after eleven p.m.** This counts double when you've been drinking.

9. **If anyone texts you after eleven p.m., you should ignore them.**

Pro Tip: *If binge drinking is breaking your budget, try running into a wall instead. Bonus: You also get some exercise.*

Hangover Cures, Ranked

AS SOMEONE WHO SPENT MORE THAN A DECADE GETTING SMASHED on a regular basis, I've had my fair share of hangovers. I also learned, through trial and error (as well as science!), some great ways to defeat the pounding in my head after a night of self-obliteration. Here's my complete list of hangover cures, from best to worst.

1. **Not drinking at all.** Yeah, you knew this one would be in there. But it's the way you prevent having a hangover entirely, so it's the number one cure.

2. **Hydration.** One of the main drivers of a hangover is dehydration. When you spend a night drinking, your body uses tons of water getting rid of the alcohol toxins coursing through it. So after every beer, shot, or drink, have a Chipotle-burrito sized glass of water. Not only does it keep you hydrated, but it slows your drinking down.

3. **Fatty and salty foods.** Drinking a lot lowers your blood sugar, which is one reason that people out drinking get serious cravings for fatty, carby foods, usually with a bucket of salt on top. So a hearty breakfast of eggs, cheese, bacon, and bread can help fix what your body needs. This is why Burger King invented the Croissan'wich.

4. **Electrolytes.** Peeing every twenty minutes during a night of debauchery leaves you salt deprived, making a hangover worse. So your body needs more of it, which you can get by slamming Gatorade or, for the most crushing of headaches, Pedialyte, which is what they give sick babies who want

their mommies to make it all better, which is exactly how you are when hungover.

5. **More booze.** Probably the worst thing you can do. But it'll help make a hangover go away. In the past I would crack open a nooner beer on a weekend to help fix the damage I did the night before. (This is also why they invented the magical thing called "brunch.") Just don't do this a lot, because then it can lead to another beer, then the bar, then another bar, then poof it's the next morning and you're hungover and now the cycle's started over again and oh shit did you really text that last night ahhhhh crap. Maybe next time just get some Pedialyte.

The Power of Good Small Talk

MOST OF YOUR LIFE IS SPENT TALKING TO PEOPLE ABOUT THE MOST boring of nonsense, especially at parties. It's called small talk, but it's also one of the most powerful ways we communicate with new people. And it doesn't have to be boring nonsense.

But first, you gotta get *into* some small talk.

1. Put down your damn phone

Stop staring at Instagram and instead look at people. See if any make eye contact and smile. That's the human version of a smiley emoji. If someone makes eye contact and smiles, you walk over, put out your hand, and introduce yourself. Boom, you just made a pal.

2. Look for groups of people who appear open

People who are standing in a circle but aren't closing the circle off are often willing to talk to strangers.

3. Just start talking to whoever is closest to you

If you're standing next to a group of people who are talking, smiling, and laughing, just turn and face them and then say these magic words, "Hi, mind if I join you?" Ninety-nine percent of the time humans at social functions are happy to be social toward strangers. So introduce yourself and start chatting.

OKAY, SURE, BUT WHAT THE HELL DO I TALK ABOUT?

After introducing yourself, see if they ask you questions. If they do, answer them! I know, sounds like rocket science, but I assure you, it's quite easy. If they don't ask you questions but continue their conversation, listen and see if there are any questions you can ask. The best thing you can do to make small talk is to ask other people questions about themselves.

THE MAGIC OF NONBORING QUESTIONS

Ask them who they know at the party. Try to ask questions related to whatever they were previously talking about. Ask each of them things about their interests, about their activities, about their lives, before revealing anything about yourself.

The longer you can get people talking about themselves, the more they will like you, because to show genuine interest in another person is an attractive trait. People love talking about themselves, and asking questions allows them to do that.

The less you talk about yourself, and the more you invite others to talk by asking open-ended questions, the more they will love you and think you're oh so cool. So keep it up. That's the best way to make small talk, and a great way to make new friends.

Hot Take: *The opposite of small talk is Big Talk, where you talk only about the classic Tom Hanks movie Big. Your mileage may vary.*

DATING
Awesomeness

They're Probably Not into You, and That's Okay

THE MOVIES HAVE LIED TO US WHEN IT COMES TO DATING. THOU- sands of terrible movies (cough, cough—romantic comedies) have been made where a love interest isn't interested in the main character. Then, miraculously, through a quirky series of events, that love interest (probably played by Katherine Heigl, remember her?) falls for our hero. The end.

That's not how it works at all. Yet, growing up, it's how I thought it should be. And I see it countless times among my friends. They think if you just keep pursuing someone, that person eventually falls for you. Nope. It's actually, uh, supercreepy. It can also make shit weird.

Before you even pursue someone, though, you gotta decide whether it's *worth* pursuing them. Or if it's even ethical to do so.

1. **Do they work somewhere you frequent?** If you hit on them or ask them out, and they have to reject you, will it make their daily life shittier because they have to see you regularly? If so, don't ask them out. (Also, as a general rule, you probably should never ask out people who you regularly give your debit card. Let *them* ask *you* out.)

2. **Do they frequently visit somewhere you work?** Again, will you make it awkward having to deal with them if you hit on them or ask them out? If so, it's probably bad news. And some jobs have rules against this stuff, so try not to get fired.

3. **Have they shown *any* interest in you?** And I mean above having to be nice to you because of social reasons. This could be because it's a friend of a friend you met at a party, and she

was being nice to you because the party wasn't superpacked and she was kinda stuck talking to you. Just because people are nice to you doesn't mean they *like* like you.

4. **If things go south, will it mess up a group of friends?** This is where you have to ask yourself if it's worth being ostracized from an entire group of people because you decide to hit on one of your friends. Romances do happen among friend groups, but is it worth messing it all up? That's up to you. (Usually, no.)

The big secret about romances is there are, in most places, a lot of people to meet. Just because you're interested in someone doesn't mean he or she is the One. (Unless that person's name is Neo. Oh god, I hope *Matrix* jokes don't make me seem too old.) So you don't need to pursue every single person who fits your criteria for being Worthy of Your Dates. Especially if it's going to make that person's world a whole lot worse.

> **Pro Tip:** A great way to tell if someone's into you is if they put your name all over their Trapper Keeper. (If you see "4eva," that means "forever." OMG, they're super into you!)

OMG, What If They're *Not* into You???

NOT ALL RELATIONSHIPS ARE MEANT TO LAST. AND IF SOMEONE IS NO longer into you, move on.

People are under no obligation to explain themselves. They're also not required to continue talking to you, to be your friend, or even to continue following you on Instagram. When they're done, they're done, and you need to move on.

Here's the exact message you should send people when they've decided they no longer want a relationship with you:

"Thanks for letting me know. I enjoyed my time with you, and I hope you find what you're looking for. Good luck!"

That's it.

Period.

Anything more isn't what adults do. Yeah, a relationship ending *suuuuuuuuuuuuuuuuuucks*, but you know what sucks more? You becoming creepy afterward. All the things that were previously cute are now generally unseemly once the other person has decided to move on. (Also, I know I've been creepy before. Nobody's perfect, but, at least I now know about my creepy behavior and I try to prevent it.)

So you need to move on as well.

Don't text exes at one a.m. Don't call them while drunk. Don't get angry and text them mean things. Don't post depressing song lyrics on Facebook, hoping they'll read them and that those lines from the Cure will win them back. When it's over, it's

When it's over, it's over.

over. Accept it, learn from it, and realize you probably had some positive times. But now you get to find someone new.

The hard truth is people become physically addicted to others. You will go through something similar to the withdrawal symptoms of a cocaine addict. That's one reason people become assholes to those they used to love. Fight that urge. Understand that, as time goes on, it'll hurt less. The more you get your heart broken, I promise you, the less it'll hurt each time.

When I was younger and got my heart broken, I wrote a lot of bad teenage poetry, which is redundant. Now that I'm in my early thirties, when something doesn't work out, I know it's not the end of the world. I was able to find someone to like me once before, and that means I can do it again. And so can you.

Quick note: If someone used to respond to your text messages superfast, and you used to have long conversations that way, then, suddenly, they no longer respond as fast, or at all, that usually means they're no longer into you anymore. It sucks, but that's usually the case. So know you probably need to move on.

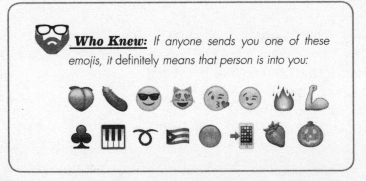

Who Knew: *If anyone sends you one of these emojis, it definitely means that person is into you:*

STOP SAYING "FRIEND ZONE"

Stop using that term. It's shitty. It's dumb. And it makes you a person no one should ever make out with. (This is a topic mostly for hetero dudes.)

"Friend zone" somehow implies a woman is wrong for not wanting to go to make-out town with you. As if *she's* screwing up, when you've been putting all this time and effort into being a "good guy." As if you *deserve* some action, because you're a "good guy." That's all horseshit.

Everyone's autonomous. No one owes you anything because you were "nice" to her. If she's your friend, that's pretty dope, and you should be happy to have friends, especially if you've got such outdated views. Also, if you were "nice" to someone just so you would "earn" the right to sleep with her, you're a bad human, and you need to jump back to the chapter called "The Asshole Test" and read it twenty-seven times.

So stop saying "friend zone." That person is your friend. You're not *waiting* to become something else. Your relationship has been defined. Being just friends with a gal is totally awesome. So stop being a shitbrain and be content with that.

Don't Be Creepy

THE MAIN THING PEOPLE DO WRONG WHEN TRYING TO FIND LOVE IS they act creepy. It comes in many forms, but it's pretty obvious when it gets pointed out to you. Here are some of the creepiest things people do, and yeah, it's mostly men who do this. I've been guilty of many of the things on this list, so if reading this makes you reevaluate your past decisions, that's good. Because now you know to no longer do them.

■ **Not taking no for an answer.** If someone isn't interested, that's that. Move on. Badgering them won't help you out. If you keep messaging them after they haven't responded to your last two messages, you're being a creep. If they change their mind (they won't), they'll let you know.

■ **Talking about someone's body.** It's always real weird when the first thing a human says to another human is about their body. Like, if you're all "Wow, you're so hot, OMG!" that's foul. Or if you specifically point out something about their body you like. A human is more than the meat shell encasing his or her brain. So don't lead off by complimenting someone's looks. That comes later, much later. Get to know them as a human and ask them questions, duh. Although, in some instances, once you have more of a rapport with someone, you *can* give them a general "You look great!"

■ **Commenting creepy shit.** No one has ever wanted to make out with someone because they wrote on a relative stranger's Facebook photo, "Wow! Looking super sexy!!! Daddy LIKES." Not once. Never. Ugh. It's so slimy. Yet it happens constantly. It's kind of like not taking no for an answer. Don't just go around creepin' on people and leaving indecent comments. Ugh.

■ **Getting super sexual superquick.** I'm a sex-positive dude, and I'm not going to judge how people communicate. But if you've just met someone, and you jump right to talking about going to "Hump Town, Population: Doin' It," it's more than likely going to creep someone out. (Also: Don't use that euphamism for sex.) So take it slow, compadre. Get to know a human before you start making sexual jokes. (And guess what, dudes? Ladies know why you make jokes like that, so you can just ramp down all the sexy talk.)

■ **Sending photos of your genitalia when no one asked.** Repeat after me: I will not send a photo of my junk to someone who hasn't requested it. Pretty simple life rule. Don't do it, fellas. And yeah, it's mostly just the fellas doing this. It's among the creepiest things you can do. So stop it. For every single time it works, it has made one thousand people feel awful. Be kind to strangers and don't send them photos of your wang.

■ **Showing up where someone works or hangs out.** This is scary shit when it happens. If someone's turned you down, then you think it's a cool idea to go where they work and "bump into" them, you're acting like an unhinged person. This is among the most disturbing things you can do. I don't care if a movie from the nineties told you this was okay. That was a movie. This is real life.

■ **Touching someone without permission.** Jesus Christ, why do I even have to say this? If someone hasn't given you consent to enter their personal space, you don't enter their personal space.

Final note: You should never do anything that makes someone feel like they're not safe. Go out of your way, if you can, to make situations seem less threatening. I'm a 6'2" muscular dude. If someone sees me walking toward them at night, it can be scary. That's why I'll cross the street or make noise when I'm walking behind someone, so they feel less threatened. You should do the same.

Hot Take: Romantic comedies are never good inspirations for gestures of love. If someone stands outside your house holding flash cards, call the cops.

How to Ask Someone Out

IF SOMEONE'S ALREADY SHOWED SOME INTEREST, AND YOU THINK they're rad as hell, you should ask them out. The best way to do it is by giving a date and time and a plan.

You say, "Are you free Tuesday after work to go out and get some tacos at Juanita's Taco Truck on Main Street?" This has a date, a time, and a place. If Tuesday doesn't work for them, they'll go, "How about Wednesday?" If they hate tacos (RED FLAG RED FLAG RED FLAG), but they're interested, then they might suggest getting Chinese food. (Unless they hate joy, other acceptable taco substitutions include pizza, burritos, or nachos.)

Also, let's—as a generation—stop asking people to "hang out." I get it, you're wishy-washy and scared of failure. But if you suggest just "hanging out," then you're communicating to the other person that you don't really know what your intentions are, or maybe you just want to be friends, or maybe you think *they* just want to be friends.

> Let's—as a generation—stop asking people to "hang out."

So, when asking someone out, use some of these phrases to show your intentions:

- ■ "Let's go on a date and get some tacos!"
- ■ "Want to go out this Tuesday and get some bubble tea then go to a bookstore?"
- ■ "Taco Tuesday sounds like a great idea for a date, let's do it!"

In every one, you're throwing out information that it's more than just two people getting together to become best friends. You're actively stating, hey, I find you attractive, and if this goes well, eventually I may try to kiss your face.

This way, if the other person isn't feeling the same, they can respond with, "Oh, wow, thank you, I think you're a real sweet person, but I'm not interested in you like that." WHICH IS A TOTALLY OKAY ANSWER FOR THEM TO GIVE, BY THE WAY. You struck out, now move on. Now you both know where you stand.

Communication is awesome. Especially in the dating world. The more you can be up-front about what you're looking for in a relationship, the easier it is for the other person to know where you're coming from. So if you're asking someone out, tell them you're asking them out.

GREAT DATE IDEAS

- Go to a bookstore. It's a great way to see what they like to read. Also, if they don't read, you don't wanna kiss their face.

- Walk around a nice public park. It puts them at ease, because you're meeting in public, and also, exercise!

- Get ice cream. Seriously, ice cream rules, and eating some with another human who you think is cute also rules.

- Get a beer at a *cool* place. Even though I don't drink now, lots of folks do, and if you're taking someone out on the most boring date ever (grabbing drinks), at least take them somewhere fancy and mysterious, like a bar in an awesome hotel or at the top of a tall building, or one with board games. (If you can get drunk and enjoy playing Monopoly, you should find a judge and get married as soon as you sober up.)

Pro Tip: *The least romantic words in the English language are "swipe" and "the doctor said it's not contagious if I use this cream."*

Make Your Dates Suck Less

THE MAIN REASON PEOPLE SUCK AT DATING IS THEY DON'T UNDER-
stand what dating actually is. It's simply a way for two people to get to know one another and decide if they groove together.

That's it. Your whole goal is to learn about another human being, and to let them do the same. It's not necessarily about having fun, even though dates *should be* fun. It's also not about making out, even though smacking lips is a great way to get to know someone.

It's all about explaining what you're into, and seeing what someone else is into. This is why going to a movie is a terrible date idea unless you're doing something else afterward.

With that in mind, here are some ways to make dates not suck.

■ **Ask the other person questions.** This is the main way to make your dates better. It's also the main way to talk to any strange person ever. You get to know someone by asking them about themselves. If you're blabbering away, that means you're not listening.

For at least the first part of any date, start by asking them about their life, where they're from, what cool shit they're working on, what they do for fun. Then smile and ask more questions.

■ **Listen to their answers and respond accordingly.** Wow, real crazy shit here, right? What I mean is you need to actually *listen* to what they are saying, instead of waiting for your turn to talk. Lots of people wait for their turn to speak instead of listening and having a conversation. Dates are about both of you. So converse accordingly.

■ **Make eye contact.** A great way to show someone you're interested is to look them in the eyes while listening. It literally connects you to what they're saying. Smiling helps, too.

■ **Controversial topics aren't actually bad.** I mean, don't open by asking them their thoughts on politics, but if it comes up, that's okay. This whole "don't talk about certain things on a date" notion is kind of bogus. If you have some serious ideological or religious issues, wouldn't you rather find out earlier rather than later?

You don't want to be six dates in only to discover they really, really despise something you care deeply about. So if a subject comes up that's usually taboo, and you seem to agree on things, might as well plow through a few other hot-button topics, while still being respectful of each other's viewpoint.

You don't have to agree on everything. But it's less painful if you know that early on.

■ **If it isn't going well, realize that's okay.** Dates don't always work out. Sometimes one of you came into it in a foul mood. Maybe they got demoted at work or their favorite plant died. Maybe your tummy hurts and this whole date is literally a pain, but you didn't want to cancel. But realize that if it's not working out, that's fine.

■ **You can end the date whenever you want.** I know so many people who have spent hours with a person they weren't enjoying instead of cutting it short and risking hurting their feelings. I think it's actually meaner to spend *more* time with a person you're not interested in, because that leads them on and makes them think things are going great when, actually, you want to bail.

I went on a date one time and within five minutes the woman just said, "Hey, so, I'm not feeling this, and I bet you think your time is just as valuable as mine, so I'm not going to waste any more of yours, and I'm going to go." She shook my hand and left. I sat there dumbfounded at just how blunt she was. But then I realized, no, she was right. I was able to meet up with some friends that night and still have a good time, and I bet she went off and did something she enjoyed, too.

This is why I suggest your first dates shouldn't be anything locked into time, so if you're not digging one another, you can bounce whenever you feel the need. If your first date is a two-hour brewery tour, and ten minutes in, your date talks about how Hitler "had some good ideas"—*this happened to me*—well, you've got another 110 minutes with Ms. Third Reich before you can skedaddle.

■ **Don't give a lame excuse if you're ending a date.** I'm going to be honest here: I used to fake excuses to leave dates with people I wasn't digging. Because my main gig has been in Web development, my thing has always been to check my phone, and then be, like, "Oh, shit, the servers are down, hold on." Then I would *go outside and pretend to make a phone call to a coworker*, all before coming back inside and saying I had to run back home and fix the servers.

See? It's insane. But I used to do it. And it "worked." But it was mean. Because it made that person think, "Oh, he's only leaving because he's having issues, not because we don't have a connection."

It's the same as leading them on. I was an asshole every time I did that. Now I just say, "Hey, I'm not feeling this." It's going to be awkward. But it's much better than me escaping and then texting them later to say I wasn't feeling it.

Be truthful and up-front while dating. A moment of awkwardness is better than inflicting any more emotional harm on a person, just because you don't want to have a quick weird conversation. That's what being an adult is all about.

■ **Make sure the other person gets home safe.** Regardless of your gender, you should give a shit about the other person making it home safe. Sometimes you meet in a strange part of town and one of you may need directions getting home. Or perhaps the area you're in isn't as safe for one of you alone. Make sure you both have a safe way to get home.

Even if the date didn't go well, unless the other person was incredibly inappropriate, you should always care about each other's safety. It's just the right thing to do.

Pro Tip: *Save messy foods until after the fifth date. And save baby back ribs until marriage. It's worth waiting for.*

Second Date Ideas

- An arcade!
- Record store!
- Go-karts
- Minigolf
- Art museum
- The zoo!
- A personalized dance class
- Laser light show!
- Model rocket building: make one together and then shoot it off
- Indoor skydiving
- Petting zoo
- How about an arcade?
- Beercade—an arcade, but with beer!
- Ice-skating
- A movie in the park when that's a thing
- Science museum!
- Group board game (double date idea)
- Winery
- Hiking
- A play
- Random wall: throw tennis balls at a wall and hit them with your hand or something
- Dog park: go and just stare at everyone else's dogs
- Fruit picking at an orchard
- Pumpkin carving (all seasons!)
- Spelunking
- Ghost/history/ architecture tour
- An arcade!

THE BEST ADVICE ABOUT LOVE

Accept the fact that most relationships fail.

There. The best advice you'll ever get about love. Pretty simple, right? We can move on, your heart will be easily mended, and ...

Yeah. Not so simple. But, in essence, it really is.

Most things fail. Not every friendship lasts. Even in your career, your business relationships can end. The same goes for romantic relationships. The grand majority of romances since the dawn of time have ended up with people splitting up.

But just because a relationship fails doesn't mean it's a failure. Odds are, you enjoyed the company of another person. You had good times. You laughed, you held hands, you smooched on couches. For some reason, you liked one another enough to give it a go.

> *Just because a relationship fails doesn't mean it's a failure.*

Then it didn't work out. Just like most things in life.

As long as you learned something and had positive times, the relationship was a success. So the next time you're with someone (or someones, no judgments here), you'll be better at it, because you learned from the previous time around.

Online Dating

MEETING PEOPLE THROUGH DATING APPS IS SUPERNORMAL. IT'S how most of my friends meet people. It's how I've been finding dates since my midtwenties. It's the new normal, so you gotta do it right.

ONLINE DATING IS NOT WEIRD, SO STOP ACTING LIKE IT IS

When you write up your profile at a site, don't say that it's strange for you to be on a dating site. That's bullshit. It's like saying you like beer but it's *so weird* you're at a bar. Everyone does it; therefore, it's not strange. I have friends who met on dating websites and are happily married. Odds are, you will meet some cool people online, too.

DON'T BE SO NEGATIVE

Whenever I see profiles where people talk about things that piss them off, it makes me think they're angry people. (And when I've gone on dates with these folks, I've almost always been right.)

You shouldn't be attacking any groups of people, or anyone's way of life, in your profile. That just makes you look petty and un-attractive. Your goal is to look attractive, so stop doing things that are the opposite.

DON'T USE PHOTOS WHERE IT'S YOU AND TEN OTHER PEOPLE

Forcing people to swipe through several photos to compare every-one in each photo to figure out which one is you is annoying. The more annoyed someone becomes when viewing your profile, the more annoyed they'll be with you. (Also, try to surround yourself with folks of an equal level of attractiveness in these photos.)

DON'T USE BLURRY PHOTOS

If your photo looks like crap, and that's what you're using to sell yourself, people won't have the best opinion of you. Use photos that are crisp and clear. Those show off your best qualities.

USE A PHOTO THAT'S A REAL REPRESENTATION OF YOURSELF

The worst thing you can do is set up untrue expectations for someone else about how you look. Don't use old photos of yourself that don't look like you now.

Every time I've met someone for a date who didn't look like her photos, I wasn't excited about it. It's bad because it's starting the relationship off on a lie. More importantly, it's robbing yourself of potential dates with people who *totally dig* how you actually look. So don't use cute angles or any other photo magic to manipulate how you look. You are how you are, and someone will like you for it.

Andy life fact: *Once I went on a date and the woman was mad because I was thinner and more in shape than I looked in my photos. She liked her men much rounder. Everyone has their preferences.*

POST ENOUGH ABOUT YOURSELF SO SOMEONE CAN START A CONVERSATION WITH YOU

If you have a profile that's relatively barren, it's hard for a person to find something to connect with and message you about. I mean, I know not everyone is looking for mental stimulation when it comes to dating apps, but it makes it easier for a stranger to talk with you if he or she knows a little about you.

BE CLEAR ABOUT WHAT YOU'RE LOOKING FOR

My fellow hetero-dudes, don't worry: Ladies know you're down to bone. Because 99 percent of the time, whenever you message a woman, the subtext is, "I want to sleep with you." So you don't need to mention that. (Also, dudes, guess what? Some women are also down to freak. That's totally okay, obviously.)

If you're looking for a serious relationship (which is also awesome!), you can mention that. Or if you're not, you can mention that, too. Communicating what you're looking for is dope. It'll help you find others who are looking for the same thing.

HOW TO MESSAGE SOMEONE PROPERLY

- Don't lead off by commenting grossly on their looks. Obviously you find them good-looking: You're messaging them. It's not only redundant, it can also be creepy.

- Don't message them anything you wouldn't want your parents to see. This is mostly for dudes. Google "bad online dating messages" and then never write any shit like that. Seriously. For every time your negging or offensive schtick where you denigrate a person worked, the other thousand times it didn't made someone feel awful. Don't do that.

- Even if you get tons of terrible messages from people, you generally don't need to screenshot them and put them on the Internet. Every person I know who does this on Facebook is consistently single. I wonder why.

- Do ask them open-ended questions based on what's in their profile. Find a way to *start* a conversation, so lead with something that allows them to open up and ask you some questions. Use words. "Hi" or "Hey, 'sup?" or any similar derivation doesn't do much for anyone.

- Show some personality with your message. If you're witty, be witty. If you're knowledgeable about something they dig, drop a little bit of that knowledge into your question.

- Don't lead off by asking someone out.

- Overall, personalize your message, make it *not* look like it's something you copy and paste to everyone you talk to. Because you shouldn't be copying and pasting the same thing over and over to everyone. C'mon, be a human and start a personal conversation.

WHAT IF THEY DON'T RESPOND?

After you send two messages with no response, move on and forget about it. Don't message that person again to see if that'll get him or her to respond. When it comes to online dating, two messages are enough.

You know what's sad? You messaging "Hi" twelve times over three months on a dating website. Don't do that.

If you start a back-and-forth and the person suddenly doesn't respond to your last message, send one more message. Continue your conversation like it's normal. Don't send anything like "Hey, where'd you go?" If the person doesn't respond to that one extra message, move on.

GET THOSE DIGITS

Eventually, what you should try to do is get the other person's phone number so you can go out sometime. Once you get to the texting stage, that's when you can set up some plans and get your groove on.

It's also so you can see how your potential new love interest is at texting. Digital communication is superimportant to most folks these days, and if a person is bad at texting, it's a buzzkill for many of us. It also helps you get a feel for someone's personality, which is also key, because it can make for a better date.

Also, when we're texting, it's easier for me to share cute photos of my cat and selfies. Part of the reason for the selfies is to reassure the person that, yes, I do look like I'm presenting myself in my photos. Not to mention, I can look silly and show off my own personality.

WHAT IF THEY STOP COMMUNICATING?

Then they're not interested. So stop texting them. Move on. When in doubt, *move on*.

Hot Take: *Online dating is like reading young adult novels: Everyone does it but nobody brags about it.*

Breakups Suck

THE FIRST PERSON WHO TRULY BROKE MY HEART WAS NAMED ROSE.
(Not her real name, of course. That would be Jennifer.) The second
was the band the Get Up Kids for their album *There Are Rules*.
Rose (again, not Jennifer) hurt more, and had more artistic merit
than that indie rock album.

When we first started dating in high school, she had left another guy to date me. I still remember being in the basement of my
house, watching some scary teen movie. We had been "hanging
out" since she left her boyfriend (who had the worst bowl cut
known to man). I didn't know if she liked me. After I mustered up
all the courage known to my sixteen-year-old body, I went in for
the only move I knew: a tickle fight.

Tickling is the only way the teenager knows how to get in the
proper position to kiss someone. I used this technique into my early
twenties, which is so shameful. I can't believe I am telling you this.
Ugh. Anywho, mid-tickle-fight, we were super close to one another's face, so I went in for a smooch. She reciprocated. We were making out. Then she was officially my girlfriend because that's all it
took in a small Nebraska town.

Having another person in your life who wants to kiss your face
was (and remains) the greatest feeling in the world. When I was
around her, I imagined it was what cocaine was like. This was Nebraska, so I never had cocaine opportunities. (We were a meth
state.) But I became addicted. Because making out with pretty humans is awesome. (After extensive scientific testing, this theory
holds true.) Then, disaster. We had been dating for maybe a month
when she stopped returning my phone calls. She had decided to
become a free agent instead of tied down to one dumb boy (me). It

hurt. It still hurts. (But not as much as that album by the Get Up Kids. What were you guys thinking?)

What I know now that I didn't know then is our brains are wired to become addicted to joy. Rose (still not Jennifer) felt better than anything else in my teenage life. She was cooler than the Get Up Kids, who had yet to release a single terrible album. When she left my world, my addicted brain freaked out. I was suffering from withdrawal. I reacted the way any addict does: begging, pleading, assholery, terrible poetry.

It took a month or two, but eventually, the symptoms stopped. I got over her. It no longer hurt when I drove past her house. (I also stopped creepily driving past her house every few days while blasting the Get Up Kids, who, as I've mentioned a few times, had yet to release *any terrible music* at this point.) My addiction to her had stopped, after those months of wishing she would come back. I no longer needed my fix. That's how it is for most people. It's also why we do crazy shit for love, like drive past someone's house every few days, hoping they'll walk outside, hear you blasting the Get Up Kids, and want to date again because of the power of music.

I've had many breakups since. It gets less painful each time. Which, in a way, is kind of sad. It means my brain is adjusting to heartache better and better. Our brains learn to adapt to the environment around us, so if you give it lots of pain it can build up a defensive perimeter around itself, closing you off to your feelings and making it so you don't have to worry about letting anyone ever hurt you because no one will want to. This is what causes some people (me) to become bitter assholes. But you can work on it. Just because someone's hurt you in the past doesn't mean everyone will hurt you in the future.

Many times in my life my heart's felt like Thor was smashing it with his hammer after wrapping it in barbed wire. (Which was also somehow superacidic?) Billions of people have felt this way. But they got through it. I'll get through it, too. And so will you. It just takes time and then your brain gets better. I promise. Just don't put your terrible poetry on a public blog that still exists more than a decade later because you forgot your password and can't delete it. Ugh.

■ ■ ■

So if you're the one doing the breaking up you need to do it with empathy. You liked this person for some reason. Now things have changed, but don't forget you were super into him or her at some point. Once I broke up with a girlfriend at her favorite restaurant. "Thanks," she told me, "now I can't ever come back here without thinking of this." So that's a bad way to do it.

One time in college, I messaged my girlfriend online and said I "needed to talk," and asked if she would come over. No sane human says they "need to talk" when they're already talking to you. It's like playing baseball with someone and saying, "I need to play baseball with you." They're going to know what's up and demand an explanation. She totally knew, and instead of talking to her in person and being more kind, I had to break up with this person I cared about in such an impersonal way—through Google Chat. That wasn't cool.

If it's someone I haven't been seeing for very long, I usually text. That message generally says this: "Hey, so I'm just not feeling this. I think you're awesome and I wish you the best of luck. Let me know if I can ever help with anything." Simple, quick, doesn't attack anyone, and ends helpful. I text this because I truly mean it. If I spend time with someone, even if it doesn't work out, I usually want to be the kind of person who would still help them in a jam.

I don't think humans are disposable once you're "done" with them romantically. That's a low way to think. Also, you never know when someone will come back into your life. For instance, Sandra Day O'Connor and William Rehnquist went on a few dates while in law school. Then they were both on the dang U.S. Supreme Court. Wouldn't it have been awkward if Sandra ghosted William and then they show up in their black robes and they gotta be, like, "Oh, uh, hey, sorry, I got busy and lost your number."

Don't fucking ghost people you're dating. Millennials just do it because other millennials do it, which is a dumb excuse for anything. It stops now. If you respect other people, you should respect people even if it's in a romantic setting and not working out. If you're texting with someone you met online, and then suddenly you're not feeling it, say so and walk away. If you go out with someone for a few weeks then aren't feeling it, say so. It doesn't need to be a huge dramatic thing. Just send a text to say you're just not feeling it. Both of you can move on and act like adults.

One hypothesis I have for why people ghost is because of how awful men are when faced with rejection. Dudes can be the worst. All I can say is, I hope men are reading this, and I hope they understand that if they're rejected, they just need to move the fuck on and deal with it like an adult. If someone rejects you, it's fine. You do not message them back and be rude. You do not attack them. You don't harass them. If someone tells you, "Hey, I'm not feeling it," your only response is, "I had a nice time with you, and I wish you the best of luck." Almost any other response is going to be icky or inappropriate or rude.

Also, rejection is normal. You are rejected thousands of times in your life, in work, in love. Not everything is meant to work out for you. That's how you grow and get better as a person. Think of it this way: Say you're playing a pickup game of basketball with friends. You miss a shot. That was you literally taking your best shot and

Rejection is normal.

the basket rejected you. Is the appropriate response to scream and shout at the hoop? Or to jump up and try to dismantle the hoop? Or to stalk the hoop on various social media networks, leaving creepy or obscene comments? Or to *threaten* the hoop with violence? Or to call the hoop a bitch or a whore or any other derogatory name? Fuck no, it isn't. So why do so many feel the need to do this with people? Sure, they're not inanimate objects. But the basic concept is the same.

Respect them, god damn it. Because if people start to do that (and by "people" I mostly mean men here), others won't feel the need to ghost all the time. And then we'll have much better relationships, even when they end.

Some of my closest friends are women I used to date. Regularly I have to ask myself, "How did I become friends with this gal? Oh, God, that's right. She was my girlfriend three years ago. Shit." They're still people I care about. Just no longer romantically. Adults treat each other with respect, even if they're no longer dating.

Adults treat each other with respect, even if they're no longer dating.

A note for dudes: In my life experience, the people who are the worst when it comes to breakups are men. They're the ones who generally are creepy, abusive, sometimes violent, and make it frightening for women during the breakup. If you're reading this book, you should know to not be an asshole when things don't work out. But if you see your male friends acting this way, *tell them what they're doing is wrong.*

Support the woman who's being treated terribly instead of your shitty friend who's being awful. Tell him he's being the worst. Sadly, sometimes men listen only when another man tells them about their behavior. So be that guy and tell a friend when he's treating someone shitty.

If he won't stop his behavior, then you need to stop being friends with him. To continue to be friends with awful and abusive people is to enable them. So stop.

Dating Myths

THE FOLLOWING IS A LIST OF THINGS PEOPLE SAY ABOUT DATING

that are bullshit.

BULLSHIT MYTH	WHY IT'S BULLSHIT
You shouldn't kiss on the first date.	That's stupid. Do what feels right, as long as the other person is down with it.
You shouldn't have sex on the first date.	Also stupid. People bone within minutes of meeting one another all the time. As long as everyone consents and you're safe, go to town.
Don't seem too eager.	You should definitely be eager to meet someone you may have a potential connection with.
You owe a person sex if you've gone out for a while.	You never owe anyone anything about your body ever.
People won't respect you if you have sex with them.	Assholes won't respect you after sex. If they're an asshole, you shouldn't date them in the first place. And that's on them, not you.
No one will like you because what you like in bed is "weird."	Everyone has different tastes and kinks. None of it is weird. It's just what you like. Odds are you can find someone else who's into what you dig.
Women don't like having sex.	lol, c'mon.
Don't text a lot because you don't want to seem too interested.	If you're interested in someone you should *want* to communicate with him or her.
I need to play games so the person will stay interested in me.	Trying to "one-up" someone is what you do when you're competing. You're trying to form a bond with a person, not beat him or her at a game of soccer. (**Quick note**: Soccer is the only thing more boring than a bad date. If you disagree, please buy seventeen copies of this book and then you can yell at me online.)

Hot Take: *My favorite dating myth is from an ex-girlfriend who said, "It's not you; it's me." Here's hoping she's more informed now.*

The Rules for Sexting

PEOPLE HAVE ALWAYS LOVED SENDING OTHER PEOPLE NAKED DEPIC-tions of themselves and talking dirty. The Egyptians made hieroglyphics of that shit. Someday, sexts will be in a museum. In old Civil War generals' letters, they're all talking fancy about how much they miss going to the bone zone with their wives.

And in our modern age, it's easier than ever to share how sexy your butt is with anyone who desires to know. But with great sexting power comes great sexting responsibility. Here are the rules to ethically sext people.

> *With great sexting power comes great sexting responsibility.*

1. Don't sext someone who hasn't agreed to it

If someone hasn't agreed to see your nakedness, or asked for you to talk dirty to them, don't do either. Pretty simple, yet so many of you don't follow this rule. Let me repeat that for the dudes reading this: *If they haven't agreed to seeing your wiener, don't send them your wiener.* It's shitty if you just flood someone's DMs with your junk without making sure it's okay. So ask! If you lack the maturity to ask, you shouldn't be sending naked photos to anyone, or talking dirty to them, either.

2. Don't forward or post anything that's shared with you

If you're lucky enough to receive some special photos someone took for you, or someone's sent you some sexy messages, don't send them to anyone else. Ever. They're meant for you and you alone.

Don't send them to friends. Don't post them online. They're yours and only yours.

3. Never share anything to shame someone else

If your relationship ends and you've got some incriminating messages that, when taken out of context, may make someone look bad, you don't share them. Whatever's sent to you during sexy times is sacred. You will *not* use it to humiliate anyone.

4. No one owes you photos ever

I don't care how long you've been dating or how you're a "good guy." No one is under any obligation to send you photos. Even if you've sent a thousand of your own.

5. You don't owe anyone photos ever

Same goes for you. If someone is badgering you about how you owe them photos, tell them to fuck off. They don't care about you if they're acting like that.

6. Never harass someone if they do or don't send you photos

This kind of goes under the standard rule of "Don't Be an Asshole," but I feel it needs to be mentioned again here because it happens so much. If you're harassing or threatening someone for photos, you're a bad person and never deserve to see a naked body ever again.

7. Sending sexy photos doesn't make you (or the recipient!) a bad person

Sexting is normal. Anyone who does it is normal. If someone tries to shame you for it, they're a bad person, not you.

8. If the relationship ends, delete the photos

After your relationship is over, get rid of the naughty photos your former partner sent you. Not only because it's the polite thing to do—those photos were generally sent because you had something going on—but also because your phone/computer/whatever could get stolen or hacked. Now those photos could be used against the person in them. That's shitty. Delete them.

> **_Hot Take:_** Sexting is like our current political process. Things can get a little weird when you add a third party.

Should I Get Back with My Ex?

Only Have "Hell Yeah" Sex

SEX SHOULD BE DOPE AS HELL. TWO PEOPLE ENJOYING EACH OTHER and gettin' all naked and grabby feely? Tons of fun. But the best sex is when everyone involved is totally into it, so that's the only kind you should be having.

This isn't about consent. (Because, obviously, you should only be sleeping with people who *can* consent and *do* consent.) But it's more about you deciding to spend your pantsless moments with people you *really, really, really* want sexy times with.

Here's a scenario: You've gone out with someone a handful of times. You're back at his or her place, smooching on the couch. Hands are roaming, blood is flowing, things are getting heavy. Now it gets to the time where sex is probably going to occur. Before you go through with it, think to yourself, are you all *"hell yeah!"* about the upcoming sex?

If the answer is yes, proceed with safety (wear condoms always, plz). If the answer is no, you probably shouldn't have sex with that person. If you're not super into it but you go ahead, you could be giving a false impression of where you're at and creating wrong expectations. Casual sex is fun and awesome. But only when you both want the same things, and when you're both super into it.

This also means if you're "hell yeah" about it, but the other person seems wary, you should stop. You don't want to have to *convince* someone who's just meh about the idea of having sex to sleep with you.

If they're not bouncing off the walls to bounce off your walls (sorry), then don't do any bouncing.

Who Knew: *Good sex is like a church service—sometimes you kneel, sometimes you stand, and sometimes it's shorter than expected.*

How Do I Know When I Should Get Married?

HOLY SHIT, DUDE. I HAVE NO IDEA. I'VE NEVER BEEN MARRIED. I'VE never even been close. But I do know this: Marriage, or any sort of long-term commitment, is drilled into us since birth as being something we should all strive for, and that's totally bogus.

You don't need to be married to be happy.

You don't need to have an "other" in your life to be happy, either.

You don't need to have any sort of relationship that defaults to whatever "normal" is as shown to us in movies, advertisements, television shows, whatever.

Whatever you want to do, whether it's get married, stay single, have twelve boyfriends at once, date no one for two straight years, it's all fine. Anyone who says otherwise is an asshole. And we don't listen to assholes.

I spent almost an entire year after I graduated college purposefully living a life where I focused on myself and didn't date. I didn't smooch any ladies; I didn't ask anyone out; I just lived enjoying myself, unencumbered by the thought of needing someone else to find happiness, all on purpose.

It was great. But more importantly, because I told myself I was doing this, I didn't have to worry about the lack of someone else in my life. I had chosen what I was doing, going against what I was taught to do. (And, partially, what most of us are biologically wanting to do, too.) I felt great.

Then I met a woman at a party, made out with her, and dated her for a long time. We're still friends (hi, Nicole!), but she didn't fill some void I felt in my life. Instead I decided I'd finally met someone worth sharing my time with. And so we did that.

Marriage isn't the right answer for everyone. Neither is monogamy. Whatever works for you, do that. If whatever that is stops working, change. Be happy knowing you're not required to live up to any of society's expectations. No matter how many times your parents tell you to get married and have kids (hi, Mom and Dad!), your life is your own to live.

MY FAVORITE DEFINITION OF LOVE: *My first girlfriend in college, back when I was a dumb nineteen-year-old, defined love for me in a way that's always made sense. She was explaining to me why she thought she loved me. Her basic reasoning: Are you willing to put yourself into discomfort in exchange for someone else's happiness? As in, are you willing to see that boring movie, or eat at that place you hate, or hang out with their awful friends, just to see the other person full of joy? If so, it means you love that person. She was right then, and she's right now.*

> **Hot Take:** *Just in case I ever get married, I'd like to take this opportunity to apologize in advance for whatever it is I did wrong. I love you, honey!*

WORK
Awesomeness

What the Hell Should You Do with Your Life?

ONE OF THE BIGGEST PIECES OF BULLSHIT THAT HAS EVER BEEN strewn about is this notion you should turn your passion into your work. If that were true—or actually possible for most of us—then the service industry would barely exist.

Let's take my dad for example. He sold cattle feed for, like, forty years. He grew up on a farm in small-town Iowa. He went to college, was drafted, served in Vietnam, did all sorts of shit. I don't think his "passion" was selling food to make cows and pigs fatter. But he did want to make a living for himself, which allowed him to enjoy other passions in life: mainly, raising a family and collecting cherry red Corvettes.

Passions are great to have. They make life rewarding. You should have a bunch. But for many of us, turning your passion into something that pays is a lifelong endeavor. Instead, you should focus on getting a decent job that *funds* your passions.

I'm a guy who grew up wanting to be so many things: a heavy metal guitarist, a punk rock singer, an opera singer, a composer, a literary highbrow fiction writer. All those things are great passions. But most of them don't help you pay rent. Or save for retirement. Or go on a vacation with someone you love.

Instead of viewing your life as chasing your dreams, view it as finding something you don't hate too much that lets you pay to make some of those dreams happen. Traditional nine-to-fives aren't awful. They usually even give you health insurance and a 401(k). Plus nights and weekends off. Which is when you can do those passions and make your life worth living.

Most of our parents didn't follow their passions. They did their best to get decent jobs and fund your eventual existence. But I bet they did fun shit on the weekends. My mom, for instance, ran her own insurance agency for almost thirty years, not exactly the most glamorous of pursuits. But in addition to being a great wife and mom, available to chaperone school trips for my sister and me, she loved music and spent a lot of free time playing piano for churches, show choirs, regular choirs, and anyone who would have her. That's the kind of life you should be striving for: one where you're financially stable, but also able to do dope shit.

With that in mind, you should be focusing on first getting a job that has these following things, which is what I call a Big Kid Job:

Full-time schedule. It should be forty hours a week, or whatever the equivalent is for where you live.

Salaried pay. Sometimes this is bad (because it means you occasionally have to work overtime without getting paid extra), but salaried positions usually mean they're more long-term.

Health care. Health insurance is one of the best things jobs offer. It depends on state and federal laws, but if you have full-time employment, it generally should include health insurance.

Vacation time. You want a job that lets you leave and enjoy your life and visit fun places. Or if you live far from home, to go back and say hi to your family on occasion.

Retirement savings. Many full-time jobs also offer matching 401(k)s, which means if you direct part of your paycheck into a 401(k) retirement account, the company will pitch in an equal amount of money, up to a certain percentage of your income (typically, 3 percent).

Yeah, superboring stuff, right? But superboring work is what allows you to lead a not-boring life.

Eventually, if you have a side project or passion that suddenly is making you so much money you need to leave your Big Kid Job, that's okay. But first, focus on getting a gig that keeps you economically and mentally stable. Otherwise your passion will be harder to make a reality.

Pro Tip: *If you can't think of anything else, become a mortician. It's the only good dead-end job.*

Why People Hire You

YOU GET A JOB BY CONVINCING PEOPLE YOU CAN DO IT WELL. THAT'S it. For some reason, this seems like a huge secret. Many people think just knowing the right people will get them a job. Or having a ridiculously great cover letter. Or wearing a sharp outfit on an interview. These are all just steps toward convincing some strangers you can get the job done.

The next few chapters are all geared toward proving you are that badass who should be employed. I've been on probably a hundred job interviews. I've also interviewed a few dozen people for jobs. At times in my career, I've had multiple job offers at the same time. (Braaaaaaag.) I've also been deep in the dumps, unable to get a job despite dozens of interviews when I *thought* I was at a great place in my career.

So I know what will screw you over. But I also know what can set you apart from everyone else. I'll also cover the basics that most people learned wrong, including me. And finally, I'll show you what to do once you get that job offer, and how to succeed in your job after you start. Let's begin, you kick-ass motherfucker you.

> **Who Knew:** Getting a good job is like hearing people laugh at your jokes. No matter how many times it happens, your father is still disappointed.

Networking Like a Not Gross Person, aka Writing Fan Letters

A LOT OF PEOPLE DON'T UNDERSTAND WHAT NETWORKING IS SUP-
posed to be. They show up to an event and hand you their card without wanting to know anything about you, or they ask what *you* can do for *them*. They come off as sleazy, and people pick up on it.

Don't be this person.

Instead, you want to do what I call building up your promotion pool. These are people who will sing your praises, because they know you're a goddamned talent. The best way to bring people into that pool is by writing one of the oldest things in the written age: the fan letter. Except, we no longer send handwritten letters anymore. We do something else.

E-mail people who do cool shit and ask them questions.

When I was starting my journalism career, I tried to e-mail three new people a week who were doing dope work. I would stumble across an article or online graphic, and then I would Google that person and see if I could find their e-mail address. Then I would send them something like this:

From: [Your Name]

To: Awesome Person

Subject: Regarding the [awesome thing they did]

Hi, there, my name is [Your Name] and I'm a [whatever you do]. I recently saw [awesome thing they did], and first of all, it was totally awesome, and I just had to tell you that.

Secondly, I wanted to know: Where'd you come up with the idea for [awesome thing]? What was the hardest part about doing [awesome thing]? And the most surprising?

Thanks for your time, and good luck in your future works!

[Your Name]

Quick and to the point. You share enough about yourself so they can get a feel for you. But more importantly, you're not asking for anything other than their expertise. So you compliment them, ask a few questions, and go on your way. In my career, I've had an almost 100 percent response rate to e-mails like these.

Early on in college, I e-mailed a reporter at the *New York Times*, one of the greatest writers the journalism profession's ever known. He e-mailed me back four days later, with kind words and praise. Most people are like that.

So you e-mail a few people every week, and sometimes, after a while, you develop a rapport with them. If they're in your city, you can ask them out for coffee to pick their brain and learn about their career. Eventually, you can ask them to look over your own projects, or maybe a résumé or cover letter, to give you career advice.

That's the way you network so it's not scummy. You're developing a relationship with another person first. Then you're occasionally asking for help, and giving help in return if they ask.

Reach out to people who are better than you and pick their brains.
Similar to when you stumble across awesome work, you should be actively looking for people in your field who are better than you. Not only so you can learn from their work, but also so you can try to ask them questions via e-mail.

Find your contemporaries and get to know them.

In whatever field you're in, others are at the same level as you. Find them, talk to them, and develop a relationship with them. The more people who know you don't suck, the better it is for you. And knowing more people means you have a wider pool of people to learn from yourself, even if they're at the same level as you.

When at a networking function, wait until *later* to give someone a business card.

Talk with others about their careers, see what they're up to, and find out if there's any way you can help them out. *That's* when you bring out your card and hand it to them.

Whenever someone has handed me their card as soon as they've met me, I've rarely ever looked at that thing again. But if it comes later in a conversation, or when we're leaving, that's when I'll actually give a damn about it.

E-mail people the next day after you've exchanged cards.

Just give them a short note that says where you met and what you do, and then say something like, "Let me know if there's ever anything I can do to help you." That's the best sentence you can include in e-mails for the rest of your life.

I always try to tell that to folks whenever I talk to them, too, because, well, the more you help people, the better the world is to you. So offer your help whenever possible.

Introduce people to one another.

Whenever you think two people will get along, in a nonromantic way, you should introduce them to one another. (You can also introduce people romantically, but this is the *business* section of this book, not the *bizness* section.) Check in with them both, and say, hey, I think you should know my friend, because you both have similar interests.

Then you send them both an introductory e-mail, describing what each person does, and let it go from there. I've been lucky in my career to occasionally get these e-mails out of the blue, and it's led me to meet superawesome people in places I've lived, and I've made some great friendships and mentors along the way.

I also remember the people who introduced us. Which makes me like them more, and makes me want to help them more. So if you do it, folks will like you more, and want to help *you* more.

> **Pro Tip:** *Networking is a lot like playing chess. Both are much more rewarding than playing checkers.*

Prove You Can Do the Damn Job

EMPLOYERS WANT TO HIRE PEOPLE WHO CAN PROVE THEY'RE CA-
pable of doing the job. If you're unable to do that, a business
shouldn't hire you.

Here's how you make yourself an awesome job candidate: *Prove
you can do the fucking job.*

You've got a handful of ways to do this, some better than others.
If you're still in college, some are easier than others, so act accordingly.

■ **Do internships.** Through internships, you'll (hopefully) not only
gain people who can recommend you later in life, you'll also get
valuable experience that *proves you can do the fucking job.*

■ **Have work examples.** If you've had an internship in which
you've completed some kind of project, you can point to this as
proof you can do the job. If not, create some real work examples on
the side. I know someone who made up a whole marketing plan for
a job she was applying for (it was a marketing position), and then
she sent it to the company as part of her application. Her application was *proof she could do the fucking job.*

■ **Write about learning to do the job.** If you're still figuring shit
out, it helps to write down your attempts at doing the sort of work
you want to do. Sure, you'll have some failures, but you'll also have
some success. And the latter acts as *proof you can do the fucking job.*

■ **Get a degree in that thing.** Sometimes you need specialized training, or certifications, to do a certain job. So get whatever instruction you need to *prove you can do the fucking job.*

COMMUNICATION SKILLS

If you're working with people, communication skills are always important. If you can't communicate that you know how to communicate, employers will communicate with you that they don't want to hire you.

So you need to do a few things:

■ **Write a good cover letter.** Your cover letter is key, because it is literally you explaining how you're a goddamn baller and can *do the fucking job.*

■ **Write a good résumé.** After they've read your bomb-ass cover letter, they're going to check your résumé to make sure you have the experience and skills needed to *do the fucking job.*

■ **Follow the proper job interview shit.** Do you follow the normal things people do when applying for a job? This means checking in a few days after applying, being courteous in your communications, and being a delight on the phone. All of these show that people will be able to work with you, thus allowing you to *do the fucking job.*

■ **Prove you're not a complete weirdo.** After you've shown you have the skills for the job and can effectively communicate, last they'll want to make sure you're not super odd. By that I mean they want to know: Are you someone they can spend eight or more hours a day with on a regular basis?

This is why in-person job interviews exist. If they call you on the phone to discuss a job after you've applied, it means they think you've proved you can do the job, so now they want to test your basic communication skills.

If you're called in for a job interview, it means they think you can do the job and you can effectively communicate, and now they wanna make sure you're not loony tunes bananas. This is where people decide if they want you around constantly, so the job is usually yours to lose at this point. (Pro tip: Don't lose it.)

SOCIAL MEDIA

It's likely your future employer will check you out online before deciding even to contact you. What shows up when someone does that? Is it a photo of you smoking a bong with a red Solo cup in your hand at Coachella? Is it a tweet documenting your messy breakup and calling someone an asshole in 271 different ways? Is it a website dedicated to talking shit about every employer you've ever had? Probably not the best first impressions. Make sure your accounts are private, or at least that there's nothing particularly embarrassing on them.

THE JOB INTERVIEW

■ **Dress appropriately.** We'll get into this later, but a lot of the job interview is decided just on how you dress. Are you following standard "office" norms? If so, you're making the case *you're not a fucking weirdo.*

■ **"Look" appropriate.** This is a lame thing, but you're going into a world that isn't as hip to how we younger folks tend to dress and look. Piercings and visible tattoos are becoming normal in the working world. But it's not always the same everywhere.

I'm of the belief that when you're starting out your career, it never hurts to look a little more conservative than you may when out with friends. So hide that septum piercing, wear something that covers the Slayer tattoo on your neck, and do whatever else necessary to make you look (I hate saying this) more "acceptable" in office parlance. This also means you should be showered and clean, too.

The more "square" you look, the more you look to many people (sadly) like you can do the job. Then, after you get the job, you slowly incorporate how you normally look back into your clothes, and if anyone has a problem with it, that's when you make a stink about it and can bring up their harassing you to HR.

You do this *after* you've gotten the job because by then you will have proved *you're not a fucking weirdo.* (Even though you are, and in this case, it's totally okay.)

■ **Don't be superstandoffish.** If you come into a job interview acting like a mean jerk, you need to be supertalented, or else people won't want to work with you. Sometimes, especially earlier in your career, you'll interview for jobs with bosses who are shitty and you just have to deal with them, because attacking them in the interview won't help you out.

Sometimes interviewers do this on purpose, to see how you respond to rudeness. (These interviewers are called assholes, by the way, and you usually don't want to work with them.) So try to be the most pleasant version of yourself, and take every opportunity to be chipper and cheerful, because it proves *you're not a fucking weirdo.*

More important than anything, in most jobs people just want to know you're someone they can spend a lot of time with. Sometimes even if you're not talented enough, as long as you're pleasant enough, they're more than willing to teach you. Try to be someone you'd want to work with, and odds are other people will want to work with you.

Pro Tip: *One time, during a newspaper job interview, I thought I'd prove I was a good reporter by telling the interviewer how much she'd paid for her house. Don't do this.*

Making Your Résumé Damn Great

YOUR RÉSUMÉ IS LIKE A DATING PROFILE. INSTEAD OF GETTING A date, you're trying to get a job interview. On both you're attempting to impress someone and convey a lot about yourself in a short space. That's why you gotta hit your résumé out of the park.

Unlike a dating profile, it's not meant to be prose. It shouldn't be a bunch of paragraphs. It's a way to quickly show your work history, your skills, and other important information in an easy-to-digest format. But most of all, it should show You Are a Badass They Should Hire. No one should read your résumé and come away wondering what it is you're good at. A résumé must show you can do the job and get results. That's why they hire you.

Here are the résumé basics:

■ **One-page limit.** If you send in a seven-page résumé, that tells your potential employer you're bad at deciding what information is important. That means you're bad at communicating, and they won't want to hire you, for good reason.

■ **Work history.** You should include every job that's relevant to where you're applying. Earlier in your career it's still okay to list part-time jobs you had during college, or even high school. As long as they show you were able to take direction and do good work, include them. But later on, these should take a hike from your résumé and be replaced by Real Jobs, aka ones that give you health insurance.

■ **List objective successes.** Show any quantifiable things you can brag about during your time at that job, usually in bullet points below a job. These help *prove* you're awesomesauce. People love seeing numbers that show success on a résumé. For example, you could say: "During my first six months at CallCo., I took twelve thousand phone calls and was 72 percent faster than the average clerk."

■ **Skills.** Somewhere you need to tell us the abilities you have that make you worth hiring. You have two kinds: soft and hard. (There's an easy joke to make here, but I won't do it, because my mom's going to read this book, and I don't want her knowing I've had sex.)

Hard skills: These deal with specific, job-based skills you have, such as operating a forklift, using Microsoft Excel, or other things that generally require training. These skills are the ones you can prove you have some aptitude with, and they're generally what you're hired for. Don't include phrases like "proficient" or "excellent" or "very good" to describe your skill levels, because they don't mean a damn thing. Just list any skills you have that you personally think you're okay at, and you're golden.

Soft skills: These are more about how you work with others and general on-the-job nonsense. They include public speaking, communicating with others, leadership and group skills, and problem solving. These aren't as tangible as kicking ass at PowerPoint slides, but they're the extra bits that make you a well-rounded employee that others want to work with. These skills usually work better as *examples* listed in the bullets under your jobs. Or by citing examples in your cover letter and *showing* these skills instead of just telling.

■ **Education.** Unless you went to Harvard or another fancy-pants college, don't put this up top. You can also list your college up top if you're interviewing with someone who went there, because people usually like fellow alumni. Otherwise put your education section on the lower portion of your résumé. Job experience is more important because the résumé is all about proving you can do the job an employer wants. You also don't need to include your grade point average unless it was *amazing*.

Not having a college degree isn't the end of the world. Same if you never even attended college. In either case, let your work experience speak for itself and don't include education at all. It may not even ever come up if your skills are awesome.

■ **References.** You must include three references on your résumé. Whenever I see résumés without any, it screams to me this person isn't confident in his ability to find others to speak highly of him. You want to make it easy for a hirer to find out more about how incredible you are. Listing references shouts, *"Check me out!"* It also saves résumé readers one step: They don't have to ask for your references. When you make their lives easier, the fewer roadblocks exist for you to get the job. Before listing anyone as a reference, make sure that person *knows* he or she could be called. You want to make sure the reference won't say anything nasty about you. I've been listed as people's reference before. But the only phone call I ever got was someone asking me for the names of *other* people who'd worked with the job candidate and me. Pretty sneaky.

■ **Miscellaneous.** I have a section on my résumé for random shit. I include colleges and conferences I've spoken at, awards I've received, and anything else I think shows I'm an asset to an employer. This is also where you can include some hobbies that show you're a well-rounded human. Your résumé should show you're not just competent at your job, but also active in other parts of your life. A well-rounded person is a desirable hire. You know, you were *Time* magazine's Person of the Year in 2006. (Seriously, look it up.)

OTHER RÉSUMÉ TIPS

1. **Design your résumé.** If you want yours to stand out, make it look different from every other Microsoft Word–looking piece of boredom. Hire someone to make it pretty. Or, better yet, learn how to design it yourself. Now you've got another résumé skill.

2. **PROOFREAD IT.** Have about ten friends look it over to find your typos and mistakes.

3. **When you e-mail it, put your name in the résumé's file name.** Résumé3.pdf gets lost on someone's desktop. Send Andy_Boyle_Résumé.pdf instead.

4. **Send your résumé as a PDF.** If you send it as a Microsoft Word file, you have no clue how old the software is they're using to read it. Do you want Bill Gates fucking up your job chances? Hell no. Save as a PDF and send it that way.

5. **Your résumé is always changing.** It's never "done," just like your career isn't. Dust it off every six months and update it. You never know when someone may want to see it.

> **_Hot Take:_** *You're going to need a résumé always. But the dream is someday your résumé will only need to say, "lol, Google me."*

Cover Letter Hell Yeahs and AW HELL NAHs

YOUR COVER LETTER IS LIKE A HANDSHAKE. IT FORMS A PERSON'S first impression of you, and the way you do it speaks volumes about yourself. And just like a handshake, it's silly that we judge a person so much based on it, but we do. (Also, it's bad if moist.) So you have to learn how to do them both well.

First, let's dispel what a cover letter is not. It's not a place for you to scream how passionate you are about the job you want. Or to say how you always wanted to be a [insert literally any job] since you were in diapers. Nor is it you just listing your entire résumé, in prose format.

A cover letter is this: the story of how you crush it in the workplace, proving that the company should hire you because of your badassery. That's it. If your cover letter isn't doing this, then you're doing it wrong.

You do these things by *showing* your talents instead of *telling* about them. This is the most important thing you can learn about writing to impress, so I'll give you a few examples:

- I'm a strong listener.
- I regularly work hard.
- Two days before the meeting with our biggest client, my boss asked me if I could restructure our entire pitch. I rebuilt it from scratch, getting input from my boss and coworkers along the way. Less than twenty minutes into our pitch, the client gave us her business, paying 30 percent higher than our normal rates.

Those first two, I am merely telling you a fact about myself. I'm just saying I am a strong listener—whatever that means—and I regularly work hard. I don't offer any examples; I don't *prove* these statements with any explanation.

In the third example, I'm not telling you I'm a good listener or a hard worker. Instead, I give a quick anecdote. My boss asked me to do something, I did it, taking notes from others, and then the project was not only successful, but we got paid more, too. What have we learned from this anecdote? I'm a hard worker (I had only two days to do the project), I'm a good listener (I got notes from coworkers and incorporated them into the project), and, most importantly, I get results (the sales pitch was a success *and* we made even more money than usual #humblebrag).

That's what your cover letter should be. You are proving, repeatedly, that you are a badass who gets results. You are *showing* your badassery through simple stories, which you can use to list your past jobs and accomplishments, showing you'd be a great fit for the company you're applying for.

You also want to show that these past skills, whatever they may be, will transition to this new job. More than anything else, the people hiring you care about how you're going to help them get what they need done.

A great cover letter has six basic paragraphs. You've got your Opening Anecdote, your Gimme the Job, your Bing, your Bang, your Bongo, and then your Closing Suck-Up.

■ **Opening Anecdote.** Your cover letter needs to start with a simple anecdote that shows you in action and makes the person who's forced to read hundreds of boring-ass, terribly written cover letters want to continue reading yours. Here's how many cover letters start: "I am writing to you about your open Accountant II position, and I believe I would be a great fit because I love accounting."

Boring and obvious. It shows you can't communicate for shit. Imagine if this opened with an anecdote: "The tax deadline was in a week, and we still had one hundred clients to go. Working at a small firm, that normally meant long nights. But because weeks earlier I'd developed a faster workflow for getting our clients' information into our system, we finished them all in just one afternoon."

It's *showing* I'm good at my job. It's *proving* if you hire me, you get a person like *this*. That's what you want to start your cover letter with.

■ **Gimme the Job.** So, using this previous made-up example, your next paragraph would be: "If you hire me as a junior accountant at BigMoneyTaxesFunTime Company, you'll get someone who's not only adept at solving complex problems, but also has a track record of innovation, saving money, and excellence."

You're stating explicitly what the job opening is, reaffirming a connection between your talents and this job opening. You're making your words echo in their minds: "If you hire me, you get this stunning person with these skills." (You're like a Jedi—you *are* the applicant they're looking for.)

■ **Bing.** This elaborates on the first of the three skills you've just listed. In my fake example, it's "innovation." Here's a possible Bing paragraph you could write: "When I was a systems engineer at NumberOneSuperOKWorldwide, after reading the manual for our software I discovered we were using a less efficient way of processing orders. So I implemented the correct procedures, and trained my coworkers on them, saving us all more than five hours of work a week."

■ **Bang.** Your next skill paragraph. For my fake letter, the skill is "saving money." An example Bang paragraph for that: "At Fake-Company Not Real LLC, I implemented a new payroll system, which saved our company more than $50,000 a year. I also streamlined our new employee induction methods from two weeks to two days, saving the company countless hours of not only my time, but also my coworkers'."

■ **Bongo.** Your final skill paragraph. In my example it's "excellence." An example Bongo paragraph for this: "My work at Accounting-PlanetBusinessPlace USA, Inc., won me the 2015 Accounting Cup, the company's highest honor. In addition to being employee of the month four times last year, I also received the Accounting America Group's gold star of excellence, which is awarded to only five accountants a year. Outside of work, I create customized bird feeders, which regularly place in regional wood-carving competitions."

■ **Closing Suck-Up.** The final paragraph of your cover letter needs to show you've done research on the company you're applying to. Here's an example: "At Tax-Job-Money-Money-Money Limited, I know you take great pride in your work, just like me. Your recent work on the Henderson estate, which won the Texas Accounting Aficionado golden calculator, is just the kind of project I could dive into. We would do some great work together. Thanks for your time."

This paragraph shows you did some homework on the company, it says you value whatever it is you found out about them, and then it says you would do well to work together. When you're researching a company, try to find some awards it has won. Or a recent project it has done that you can critique positively and with specificity.

■ **Here's the biggest secret about cover letters:** You *should* be copying and pasting most of it, over and over. Odds are, you've chosen a career in a certain field. So your cover letter is pointed toward a specific type of company. That means you shouldn't need to rewrite it over and over and over. Instead, you should be working on one super marvelous cover letter, with sentences you can fit to the specific company.

In the Gimme the Job paragraph, you're stating the name of the company and the job title. In the Closing Suck-Up paragraph, you just put in whatever information you researched about the company. These are kind of the Mad Lib sections, where you pop in the names of where you're applying.

OLD ADVICE THAT'S WRONG

1. Write a new cover letter per job. Hell no. Each time you do this, you have more potential for errors. Use the basic cover letter format I mentioned earlier, then change up the Gimme the Job and Closing Suck-Up paragraphs to fit the job you're applying for.

2. Include the address and name of the company at the top of your letter. They know what their company is and where it's located. Don't do this.

3. Address your cover letter to the hiring manager. Many people will see this, not just the hiring manager. So you don't need to make your letter "Dear [Whoever]." Just start your Opening Anecdote and you're fine.

4. Put the date at the top. When you do this, you've forever given a stamp to your letter that makes it look old. People don't like dated shit. If you have no date, it looks timeless, like Helen Mirren. Don't include one.

5. Don't use links in cover letters. Most people read your cover letter via their computer, so they *should* have links they can click on that prove your badassery, if it exists.

COVER LETTER HELL YEAHS

■ **Do include your contact information at the bottom.** Sometimes these cover letters and résumés get printed off and passed around an office, even though they came in via e-mail or some Web application system, and this information gets lost. Keep it on both documents and you'll be fine.

■ **Do brag if it's a claim you can back up.** You can be humble yet still boast about your accomplishments, so do it.

■ **Do tell the truth.** You shouldn't have to lie to sell yourself. So never lie. Always tell the truth on a cover letter. This is why you should use things you can *quantify*, because these are facts you can always back up.

■ **Do have multiple people read your cover letter.** The more eyes you can get on your cover letter, the more advice you can get. More importantly, the more chances you'll have to catch your grammar mistakes and typos.

■ **Do show your personality.** Your cover letter should show you're not just a badass, but also a human. It's fine to include a few sentences about your hobbies, even if they don't show you as some amazingly creative person. If you like to bowl, include it. If you're active in your church choir, do it. A competitive bodybuilder? Cool shit! Show you live an interesting life, because hobbies show you're attempting to make yourself a better person, which is the kind of employee most places want.

■ **Do ask former coworkers about your work.** You don't remember everything, which is why you should ask people you used to work with what good work *they* remember you doing. If it stuck in their brain, it's probably worth noting in your cover letter.

■ **Do let the cover letter sit for a few days before sending it.** Even after you've edited it multiple times, gotten feedback from others, and revised it again, give it a day or two to just sit. You want to look at it with fresh eyes.

■ **Do send the cover letter as a PDF.** Just like the résumé, save it as a PDF file instead of a Word-equivalent file. And give it a name like Andy_Boyle_Cover_Letter.pdf, too. If you're e-mailing your cover letter to someone, you should copy and paste the contents of it in the e-mail. Then attach your résumé and the pdf version of the cover letter, too. Say something at the bottom of your e-mail like "I've attached a copy of this letter, as well as my résumé, to this e-mail."

COVER LETTER AW HELL NAHS

■ **Don't use fancy-pants words.** You're not writing a term paper meant to impress an English professor who never got his or her novel published, so don't act like you are.

■ **Don't send out a hundred cover letters at once.** Instead, when applying for jobs, use your cover letter for just a handful of jobs at a time. Send it out in batches of five to ten places. What you're doing is testing the waters, making sure this cover letter doesn't completely stink. If you have a decent cover letter, and most of the required job qualifications, you'll hear back from a few places. If it sucks, no one will respond, and you can adjust accordingly.

■ **Don't apply for jobs that require you to mail in a cover letter.** If they're this behind the times on their hiring practices, think of what else they're behind on.

■ **Don't name-drop in the cover letter.** If you have such a big connection you think it'll help you get called for an interview, instead you want that connection to e-mail the hiring manager directly with a copy of your résumé and cover letter. That way, they know who it's coming from. No name drops needed.

■ **Don't talk about overcoming a personal tragedy.** This isn't a college entrance essay. This is a cover letter for a job. Instead, talk about overcoming an obstacle at work.

A note for women: Even though it sucks a lot, if you're trying to get pregnant (or are recently pregnant), do not tell that to an employer. Some would say this is withholding information, but it's not an employer's business to know that in nine months you're potentially going to need maternity leave. That's something to deal with later, after you've gotten the job, when you actually *need* maternity leave.

What also sucks (again, I'm sorry, the world can be awful) is that women wearing an engagement ring have less of a chance of being hired. Older people hiring you assume you only want the job until you "get married and start popping out kids," rather than being serious about your career. (A real thing I've heard at an office.) This is ridiculous, but it happens, because the world is often (no surprise to you) shitty to women.

Now, there's a chance you wouldn't want to work for assholes like this anyway, but if you're trying to get into certain fields it could be an issue. It's not about deceiving anyone. It's about not letting their terrible, misinformed notions dictate whether or not you get a fair chance to do the damn job.

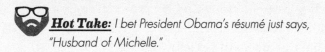

Hot Take: *I bet President Obama's résumé just says, "Husband of Michelle."*

Don't Wear Cologne or Perfume to an Interview

CUCUMBER MELON IS THE WORST SMELL IN THE WORLD. WHENEVER it hits my nostrils, I'm instantly transported back to junior year of high school. A girl I dated pops into my brain. Because that's the scent she wore every time we hung out. Now when I smell it, I'm reminded of heartache and the terrible songs I wrote about her.

That's the power of smell. The cologne or perfume you wear can evoke strong emotions and memories. Especially the ones that are mass-marketed and sold to millions. I think every other man has worn Ralph Lauren's Polo at one point in his life. Which means lots of shitty people have worn that scent. So if you wear it, you'll remind everyone around you about that jerk they used to know who bathed himself in it. And now they'll relate you to him, and now you're also perceived as a jerk. (I stopped wearing Ralph Lauren after a woman in college told me it reminded her of an ex who peed in sinks. I no longer wear cologne at all, because you don't need it.)

If you wear deodorant and shower regularly (at *least* once per day, please), your body will smell pretty good during a job interview. But watch out with strong-smelling deodorants: Some of them can do the same thing as those terrible perfumes and colognes. If you stick with going fragrance free, you won't accidentally remind anyone of something terrible when you sit across from them during an interview.

I mean, sure, you *can* wear cologne or perfume. Or both! Live your life. Just know that when you do, there's a chance someone will think, "Wow, you smell like someone I hate." It's dumb but we do it.

Pro Tip: If you accidentally break your glasses before an interview, you should probably just not wear them, because who in their right mind would fix them with painter's tape and then go meet a potential employer? (I did this.)

Always Negotiate

YOU DON'T GET WHAT YOU DON'T ASK FOR, SO IF YOU GET A JOB offer, or if you get almost anything in life, always negotiate. Always ask for more money than they offered. Always ask for more vacation time. See if you can get even more perks. Then get it in writing in an official offer letter. This way everyone is on the same page. (And so they can't screw you over when you show up and they're, like, "Uh, sorry, we're paying you half as much.")

Most managers expect you to negotiate, because that's how it works. It also shows you're assertive and, in their eyes, it says you'll probably be a stronger employee. (And one they can't fuck around with as much, too, which is good for you.) If they say no to things, that's fine, too. Generally, they'll compromise and give you part of what you want.

People's biggest fear is they'll take the job offer away if you negotiate. If they do that, they're assholes. Do you want to work for assholes? In most cases, nope. So always negotiate.

> **Hot Take:** If you're ever required to fill out an online application and it asks for your expected salary, just write "$1 million." Partially so it forces them to come up with an appropriate salary figure for you, and partially because if they hire you for less than $1 million, it's totally a steal!

Develop the Reputation You Want

WHAT YOU'RE STRIVING FOR IN YOUR PROFESSIONAL—AND personal—life is to have people say these magical words about you: *You're nice and dependable.* That's what humans are looking for in you, whether it's at your job, at your rec softball league, or when you're going out with someone. You want to be nice *and* dependable.

DEVELOPING A REPUTATION FOR BEING NICE

This means you're pleasant to be around. I'm not saying you need to be some outgoing giggle monster. I'm also not saying you need to ask everyone how they're doing and high-five them and seem deeply interested in their every word.

But you do need to make an effort to engage with others pleasantly and not say mean things. This means you're not acting like an asshole (see "The Asshole Test") and you're trying to be extra helpful whenever possible.

1. Don't be shitty in e-mails

Whenever you're rude in writing, it can be forwarded to anyone else, proving your shittiness. You shouldn't be mean in general, but if you feel like you gotta take someone to task, do it in person. They can't forward a one-on-one conversation to your boss.

2. Don't correct someone publicly

Many times in my career during meetings I would correct people when they were wrong. My bosses started to view me as an asshole. I was invited to fewer meetings and given less responsibility because of it. If someone is wrong and it's not the end of the world, correct the person later in private. It's the nonasshole thing to do.

3. Correct people nicely

If you do have to correct someone, say it in a way that makes it seem as though the person *knew* the right answer, but *accidentally* said the wrong thing. "I think you may have misspoken when you said [totally wrong thing]" is a great way to do it.

4. Always give everyone else credit

If anyone ever compliments you on work you did, always mention every other person who worked on it and say *they* are the ones who deserve the true credit. *Even if you did the entire damn thing yourself.* Spreading credit around endears you to everyone else. It's also just a nice thing to do. Not to mention, no success happens in a vacuum. Others helped, even if you don't *think* they did.

5. Brag the right way

If you want to brag about a project you did, what you should do instead is thank everyone who helped you on the project. Throwing up an accomplishment about yourself on social media is icky. Thanking others who helped you achieve that accomplishment? Aces.

6. Just try to be pleasant

When in doubt, be kind. That should be how you live your life anyway. But the work world can get stressful. Don't add to it by being a shithead.

DEVELOPING A REPUTATION FOR DEPENDABILITY

You want to become the go-to person for your bosses. That's how you get recognized on the job, get raises, get better job responsibilities, all that fun stuff. You do that by *proving* you should be that person. It takes time, but here's how you do it.

1. Never do just the bare minimum

Always go beyond what's asked of you. If you think something else needs to be done, just do it, and don't ask for acknowledgment that you did it. If you're working on a project with your coworkers, and you've noticed someone's slacking off, instead of pointing it out to them, just do the work and get it done. The more you do these sorts of things, the more folks start to notice *you* are the one always picking up the slack.

2. Let others notice your hard work

Don't bring up all the extra work you're doing. Bragging about doing your job to the best of your ability is no good. Your dependability should always speak for itself. By bragging about it, you're not being nice.

3. Make doing good work its own reward

When you're dependable, it becomes its own reward. It leads you to better opportunities. Eventually people realize you're a bad-ass dependable human and they want you around. Remember that kid in high school who you were always superexcited about doing a group project with? That's because that kid was dependable (and probably nice, too). You want to be that person.

4. Volunteer for the shitty assignments, then do them amazingly

If you kick ass on the work no one else wants to do, it'll show your superiors you will *definitely* kick ass on the harder projects. That's why if no one else wants to do something, raise your hand and say, "Hell yeah, I'll do it."

5. Never leave it at "I don't know"

If your boss asks you about something, instead of answering, "I don't know," you should *instead* say, "I don't know, but let me see if I can find out." Or "I don't know, but I think XYZ is on that project—want me to connect you two?" Whenever you don't know the answer, speak up and then say you'll do your best to figure it out.

Be nice. Be dependable. Because that's how you become successful.

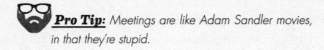

Pro Tip: *Meetings are like Adam Sandler movies, in that they're stupid.*

Dressing for Successing

I NEVER CARED ABOUT FASHION UNTIL THE LAST FEW YEARS. I JUST wore whatever plaid shirt I could find that didn't smell, put on an undershirt (it didn't matter if it clashed with the plaid, obviously), and then wore ill-fitting jeans with sneakers that may or may not have had stains on them. This was my standard outfit for years.

And people, naturally, judged the hell out of me because of it.

Now, it wasn't like they would come up and say, "You are dressed like shit." (Although one newspaper editor asked why my shoes were duct-taped, and I told him, "Because you don't pay me enough to afford new shoes." I zinged us both real good.)

But if you're dressed like a slob, people assume you're kind of dumb. If you're dressed like you don't give a shit, people don't give a shit about you. The way I dressed was telling the world, "Hey, I don't care about myself. So neither should you."

Whenever you go out in public, or to work, you should always give a shit about the way you dress. This doesn't mean you need to wear a Hugo Boss suit and tie or Prada shoes. But it does mean you need to care. Here are some basic strategies to help you look like you give a shit:

1. Have clothes that fit.
2. Wear clothes that match.
3. Invest in the staples, or what you wear every day.
5. Don't be *too* showy.
6. Always dress like you're two hours away from meeting the love of your life.

7.　Once you find your style, stay with it.

8.　If you feel uncomfortable in your clothes, others will notice.

9.　Dress one level nicer than you think you should.

10.　Always have nice and clean shoes.

Sure, some people can break these rules. Lots probably can. These people are called "fashionable" and they're amazing. But generally, many of us don't know how to dress ourselves. These basic rules are meant to help, not to make you feel bad for how you already dress. I'm not saying you must follow these guidelines or that you're bad if you don't. But until your friends are regularly complimenting your style and fashion sense, it's smarter to stick to the basics. Surprisingly, the more boring you dress, the better you tend to look.

Pro Tip: *Imagine someone who looks cool. Notice how that person is not wearing a Bluetooth earpiece? Lesson over.*

Things You Think
Matter at Your Job but Don't

- Nobody remembers if you didn't eat any of the cake during someone's birthday party.

- Nobody cares if you go for a run or to the gym during your lunch break.

- Nobody remembers that you didn't go out with everyone for drinks that one time.

- The ability to wear jeans on Friday doesn't mean your office is cool. It just means four days a week you have to wear clothes that probably need dry-cleaning.

- Nobody cares if you don't sign that card for someone's birthday, retirement, baby, promotion, or whatever.

- Nobody remembers how often you work with new people.

- Nobody cares where you sit.

- Nobody remembers what you ordered when you all went out for lunch.

- Ping-Pong tables at cool offices are rarely actually used, because people expect you to get work done at your job.

- Nobody cares which neighborhood you live in.

- Having beer in the office you can drink whenever usually just means more of your coworkers (or yourself) will drink too much, which isn't a good thing.

- Nobody remembers if you had to leave work early that one time.

■ Nobody actually expects you to check your work e-mail when you're on vacation.

■ Nobody is going to judge you for not coming to work when you're sick, and they'll probably thank you for keeping your germs away.

■ A fully stocked kitchen doesn't make your job cool. It usually means they just don't want you leaving the office, so you can be more productive. Same goes if they have showers.

■ Nobody expects you to be best friends with everyone at the office.

■ Nobody will ever care about your upcoming improv show.

Things You Think Don't Matter at Your Job but Do

- How clean your shoes are.
- How you write e-mails.
- The strength of your handshake.
- Your work doesn't always speak for itself, so sometimes you need to be your own advocate.
- Playing "the game" of office politics.
- Your placement of your food in the fridge, blocking off other people's food, thus making them hate you for having to move your food two inches to get theirs.
- Office gossip.
- How messy your desk is.
- Signing the card for Barbara's baby shower with anything other than "Congratulations!"
- Never showing up to any work social outings.
- The fact that you went to a college that has a sports team someone else hates.
- Failing to watch last night's episode of *Game of Thrones*.

Should I Sleep with Someone I Work With?

NO.

Making Friends with Coworkers

THE OFFICE IS SOMETIMES A WEIRD PLACE FOR RELATIONSHIPS.
You're around these people all the time, and of course you may start
to become pals with some of them. It's totally natural you'll want to
hang outside of work. But you want to make sure you maintain
some boundaries with your work friends.

■ **Don't do drugs with them.** Yeah, I know, this seems obvious,
but, hey, people sometimes do drugs with their friends. That's just
fine. But try to not do them, or even talk about doing them, with
your coworkers. You never know where people's boundaries are,
and they may find your joint smoking so objectionable they tell
HR. It happens, so don't let it happen to you. (Also, just thought I'd
point out that you should always follow your local laws regarding drugs and alcohol, regardless of what you read in a silly advice
book.)

■ **Do go out for drinks with them.** But don't get *too* drunk. Coworkers go to bars after work all the time. It's a form of networking. So
knock a few back on occasion. Try to make sure you keep yourself
from becoming a total jackass, by limiting how much you drink. If
you limit it to two before you head home, you'll probably be just
fine.

■ **Don't just bitch about your job with them.** Sometimes hanging
out with your coworker friends outside of work just turns into complaining sessions. Sure, a little bit is good and therapeutic, but if

you realize all you ever do outside of work is talk about work, it's going to make you resent your job. I used to do this when I was younger, until I realized most of my waking hours were spent either *at* work or with coworkers *talking* about work. My brain never escaped, so I began hating my job because of it. Try not to fall into this trap.

■ **Don't sleep with a coworker.** Seriously. Just don't do it. Remember how awkward it was in high school when you made out with that cute classmate and then it didn't work out but then you had two more years of seeing one another in the halls and then, ugh, had to do a team class project together in your American history class? Imagine that, but now it's someone you spend forty hours a week with. Not to mention, most relationships fail, and odds are, your work one will, too. Oh, also sometimes it's a fireable offense to have a relationship and not disclose it to your boss, so are you really comfortable telling your boss about how you and this coworker are grinding outside of work hours? Just find someone else to lock lips with. It's for the best.

> *Most relationships fail, and odds are, your work one will, too.*

■ **Be personal, but not *too* personal.** For starters, don't talk about your dating or sex life with coworkers. At worst, this is considered sexual harassment. At best, you're probably making someone else feel uncomfortable. So don't do it. And people are into different things. Try to keep politics and religion out of your work conversations, too. Not everyone is going to want to come to your church's fish fry or Friday's rally to stop the governor from eating endangered rhinos or whatever. You're a professional, so even though you're friends, you need to stay professional.

Who Knew: The terms "work husband" and "work wife" were invented because someone wasn't allowed to adopt any more cats from a shelter.

Don't Get Burned Out

EARLY IN MY CAREER, I DIDN'T KNOW WHAT A WORK-LIFE BALANCE was. All I did was work. I put my time in at the office every day, and then as soon as I left, I spent more time trying to become better at my job. On the weekends, same thing. It was what my brain spent most of the time doing—thinking about ways to become a better employee.

Then my brain exploded and I began hating everything about my job. I snapped at people. I started dry-heaving before work, sick that I would have to be there. My productivity dropped and I spent all my free time complaining. I was a mess.

I was burned out, because I never truly developed healthy hobbies. I hadn't learned how to turn my brain from "work mode" to "Andy fun fun relax time fun fun mode." I've since learned how, and I found the best way to do that is to make clear boundaries with your employer about your free time, and then to find fulfilling things to do with that time.

■ **Setting boundaries.** If you work a normal nine-to-five, odds are your work is done when you leave the office. Sure, sometimes emergencies happen and things go haywire and you have to work late or on the weekends, but when you get a salaried job, you normally work a steady week. Even if you work in a more time-intensive occupation, you still need to carve out time for yourself, and you need to let your employer know that.

Earlier in your career, they'll probably work you harder, because you're young. They assume because you may not have a family or kids or other big responsibilities, they can treat you this way. It's bullshit, so you should call them on it, once you've developed a good working reputation with your employer. You need to make sure that they aren't always hounding you after you leave the office. Because if you start letting them do it all the time, they'll develop a habit of doing it all the time.

Which is why you need to have these conversations about your work-life balance with your boss if you're ever starting to feel burned out. Or, better yet, it should be discussed earlier, while you're still interviewing for the job. Let the employer know you value your free time, because the less stressed you are, the more productive you are during work hours.

Which is actually true: If you're not freaking out about work, you work better. They want you to be a good little worker bee, so explain to them that while you understand emergencies come up, they should respect your off-hours, just like you respect your on hours by trying to be the best staff member possible.

■ **Developing hobbies.** Having shit to do after work is good for its own reasons, and it also allows you to signal to your bosses you'll be busy and that they can't actually ask you to do anything. So find some activities to do after work. Maybe you developed a love for Dungeons and Dragons in high school. Perhaps you want to join a recreational soccer league. Or maybe you just like writing self-help books and detective novels. All are great ways to exercise your brain and body, and you should develop a few.

The more things you do outside of work that aren't related to your job, the more you'll feel refreshed when you go into work. Because your brain is spent doing all these different activities when you're outside the office, you'll almost get excited to tackle your work-related problems, even if it's just staring at spreadsheets all day. Also, you train your brain to go into "work mode" by learning how to turn it off after work. So it knows the difference between you being in "play mode" and "work mode." This will help with your productivity, and it'll make you a happier human.

Some hobbies can open your brain up to new career paths, or even new job opportunities. Maybe you join a local soccer league, and one of your teammates works somewhere you'd like to work. Now you have a person who's got an in there. You can also learn new skills, which could apply to your current job, or a future job.

If one of your hobbies is writing short fiction pieces, that'll help with your overall writing and communication skills. If you're into bird-watching (seriously, I have friends who do this shit), that'll teach you not only about patience, but how to deal with something superboring (ha ha ha, I kid, but no, really).

Doing Professional Thangs

IF YOU'RE A PROFESSIONAL, YOU NEED TO ACT LIKE IT IN MOST OF your public doings. That mostly means you should learn how to communicate like a professional. And the main way we communicate these days is through e-mail and phone calls, as well as GChat and Slack in some offices.

Here's an e-mail that isn't professional:

> **Subject:** Yo dude sup?
>
> **Text:** hey dawg waddup? hope u fools are doing great over at BroCo, lol. anywho, i was wondering if u got those files I faxed over? if not, no biggie, just get back to me asap, thanks bro.
>
> smell ya later,
>
> > big dawg

Yeah, like, obviously this e-mail sucks. I mean, I would maybe jokingly send this to a close friend. I also would pick a better signature than "big dawg," let's be honest here. But more importantly, in an e-mail like this, you're not acting professional because you're writing too informally.

That doesn't mean your e-mail has to be boring and lame. But it does mean you need to come off like you give more of a shit than Big Dawg up there. Here's a better version of that e-mail:

> **Subject:** Checking in on the Anderson files
>
> **Text:** Hey, Dana,
>
> It's Andy from CoolAwesome Company, Inc. We talked yesterday about the Anderson files. I faxed over the ones you requested yesterday around 3 p.m., and I'm just checking to make sure

someone over there received them. Let me know if you need anything else, or if you need me to fax them again. Thanks for your help!

> Andy Boyle
> Head of Compliance
> CoolAwesome Company, Inc.
> (555) 555-1234

See how this is formal, but it's not too boring? The subject line gives the reader the gist of what this e-mail is about. I introduce myself, which you should always do if there's even a possibility that they may not know who you are. Then I say what I need from them, which is to know whether or not they received the files (and I give the time I faxed them over), and to contact me if they need anything else. I also say thank you at the end.

It's respectful and short and it gets across everything I need it to. Then, my e-mail signature reiterates who I am, my position, where I work, and a direct phone number to reach me. Notice how it doesn't have a dumb quote about success? Because including quotes in e-mails is for the worst humans. Don't be that person.

E-mail rule: Don't ever use a crazy font. Don't ever use Comic Sans. Don't have a superlong signature that also features a quote about success, a quote from the Bible, or a quote from yourself. (I have seen all of these, sometimes multiple in the same e-mail.) Also, don't change the color of your e-mail text to something on the Crayola spectrum. What color is the text in this book? That's right: black. Stick with it.

Don't ever use Comic Sans.

This is also how you should e-mail people you work with. Have a formal tone, but not too weird and stern. When in doubt, err on the side of being boring and formal rather than informal. You never know who your e-mail could get forwarded to, or how something you say might be taken in the wrong way.

Another place you need to be professional is in phone calls. When you're calling someone, and let's say his name is Robert, here's how it *shouldn't* go:

"Hey, Bobby! Bobby boy. The Bobster. Bobman! Bob Bob Bob, Bob Bob Bobman! Hey, it's Andy over at CoolAwesome Company, Inc.! What the fuck is *up*, my man! Anywho, just calling to check in and see if you need any more shit from us. You good, bro? You good? What's the dealio?"

I have received phone calls like this from people I do not know that well. It is jarring. It isn't fun. It makes you sound like you're some slick eighties salesperson who uses phrases like "busting balls." Ewwwwwwww. Don't be this person.

Instead, be *this* person:

"Hey, Robert, it's Andy over at CoolAwesome Company, Inc. Just calling to check in and make sure you got everything you need from us. Anything else we can do?"

And then you shut up and listen to Robert's answer. And then you help Robert. That's all you need to do. Pretty simple.

OTHER PROFESSIONAL SHIT

- Send thank-you cards. I remember every thank-you card I've ever received, even when it was from a coworker who I helped out on a project.

- Don't swear in the office until you've heard your superiors use swear words ten times. That earns you one public swearword.

- If you're representing your company at something, know that you are an embodiment of the firm and should be on your best behavior. This means if you're at a conference, don't get too drunk. Don't hit on anyone. And in general, don't be an asshole.

- Check up on things regularly, but not every hour. Do not be the person who sends an e-mail to a coworker and then immediately walks over to their desk to make sure they got the e-mail you sent *two goddamn minutes ago*.

- Use less jargon. Use words that actually mean shit. Don't say "synergy" ever. Don't you dare say "think outside the box." Etc.

- When in doubt, think what an asshole would do, and then do the opposite.

General note about work computers: It's a good rule to never leave anything personally important on a work computer.

1. It's a dangerous idea, because work computers are usually old and crappy and can break at any moment, and then all those photos of your niece learning to crawl you saved are gone forever.

2. If you get fired or escorted immediately out of the building for any reason, that only copy of the novel you've worked on for ten years during your work lunch breaks is now lost to IT hell.

3. You never know who could be snooping on your computer while you're gone, and leaving personal things like that makes it easier for someone to steal your identity, among other things.

Pro Tip: *If you ever accidentally hit Reply All on a company-wide e-mail, your best choice of action is to move to Siberia. Don't send a group e-mail to say good-bye.*

BODY
Awesomeness

Exercise and Eat Less Crap: You'll Feel Better

I WAS ALWAYS A CHUBBY KID GROWING UP. MY MOM WOULD SAY I was "husky," because I guess it's nicer to be called fat when it's also a breed of dog. So I've tried to get in better shape probably a dozen times in my life.

Most kids I knew were bone thin, so even though I was just a little overweight, I was monstrous in comparison. Early on, I tried diets in high school. They never worked. I would always relapse, going back to my old habit of pizza, Taco Bell, and crushing teenage regret.

What finally worked was realizing this wasn't something I was going to do for a few months to shed a handful of pounds. I needed to rethink my entire relationship with food. I needed to change the way I consumed it, and what I was regularly putting into my body. It wasn't a diet; it was a lifestyle.

Here's what I've learned about exercise and eating healthy. (FYI: I'm not a doctor, so you should always check with one before starting any new strenuous activity to make sure your body's capable of doing it.)

CALORIES IN, CALORIES OUT

If you eat less food than your body needs, you lose weight. If you eat more than it needs, you gain weight. If you eat just the amount it needs, you stay the same. Science has proved this over and over again. I've personally proved it many times over.

Your body is always trying to maintain homeostasis. It's trying to always stay the same, just like a teen pop star. So it needs fuel to run and make energy. (Also like a pop star.) Give it less fuel than it needs, and it needs to find that fuel elsewhere. Which means your body will, well, eat yourself. It's like an ouroboros, except less snaky.

I lost a bunch of weight by eating less than my body needed. Conversely, guess how I gained all the weight in the first place? By eating too much!

MOVE MORE!

Exercise is awesome. Most of us aren't doing it enough. When I say exercise, I do not mean you have to go run eighteen marathons this week. (If you can, you can probably skip this chapter while you're icing your calves.) I basically mean you should just move your body more.

For me, I like lifting weights and walking a lot. Previously, I wasn't doing either. So now I'm moving more, and thus exercising my body more. Find what works for you.

The more areas of your body you can exercise, the better. You don't have to go to a gym and lift weights. You can go swimming. Or rock climbing. Or play a pickup game of basketball or baseball or soccer or curling. (Wow, now I want to find a curling league.)

The main thing you should be doing, though, is always trying to push yourself a bit more than you were doing before. If you walk for twenty minutes, walk twenty-one minutes the next time. If you were able to bench-press one hundred pounds ten times, try benching one hundred pounds eleven times.

Because of that homeostasis thing I mentioned earlier, if you push your body a little extra every time you exercise, it'll adapt and get stronger. Which leads to an overall healthier you.

DRINK MORE WATER!

Most of us aren't hydrating ourselves enough. Doctor's say you should be drinking, in ounces, your weight divided by two. As a guy who weighs about 220 pounds as of this writing, that's a lot of water.

I pee. Constantly. Like, all the time. But being hydrated keeps my mind running better. It also keeps my mood better regulated. My body stays at a good temperature throughout the day. And it seems to help me digest food better. (Now you know I poop!)

Sometimes your body tells you, *"Feed me now"* when actually it's trying to say, *"Please, I would like water."* Your brain wires get messed up, so you go eat food when actually you're thirsty. If you're staying hydrated, it'll help keep your internal hunger games at bay.

EAT MORE PROTEIN!

Your body uses protein to build and maintain muscle. Not to mention, protein helps to keep you feeling full. If you increase your protein intake, you'll generally feel less hungry throughout the day.

I drink protein shakes to help me hit my protein goals, which are higher than the average person's because I lift weights a lot. But because of the amount of protein I eat, I am rarely hungry. When I used to eat a diet that consisted of more carbs, I'd be hungry an hour after I ate.

EAT FEWER BAD CARBS!

Carbs are not bad, despite whatever the latest magazine fad diet has told you. The problem is our diets generally contain carbs that aren't as healthy for us. Good carbs come from dense vegetables—think broccoli, cauliflower, sweet potatoes. They fill you up and take a while to digest, so they keep you from getting as hungry. And they aren't as rich in calories.

On the other end of the carb spectrum are sugary foods, such as candy, soft drinks, and ketchup (I know, right?)—or things such as bread that break down into sugars—that pump up the insulin in your body. You know that crazy boost you get after eating a candy bar? That's your insulin spiking in your blood.

Then you know that crash you get a short time later? That's because the insulin dropped from your blood suddenly. It makes you want to just sit on the couch and binge watch *Game of Thrones* and wish Bran actually did something. We've all been there.

These are the kinds of carbs you should avoid. Sure, the occasional sugary delight is great. (French macarons are a big reason I go on living.) But, like all things, in moderation.

Fun fact: Your brain responds to sugar the same way it does to cocaine. That's why we love the shit out of sugar. It's a habit that takes a while to beat.

SLOW WEIGHT CHANGE IS GOOD!

If you're trying to change how much you weigh, the slower you do it, the more likely it is that you'll not only hit your goals, but also stay at that new weight.

If you're trying to lose weight, you should aim at losing, at most, two pounds a week. One pound a week was my goal for about a year, and I hit it pretty consistently. Think of it this way: If you're overweight, you didn't gain all those extra pounds in a week. So you're not going to lose them all in a week, either.

Same goes if you're trying to gain weight. If you want to bulk up, do that slowly, too. It'll help you gain more muscle and less fat.

SET SMALL GOALS!

Regardless of your health goals, make them small. If you're trying to run a mile in under nine minutes and your current speed is twelve, you'll feel bad because you're so far from your goal. Instead, make your goal to run a mile in eleven minutes and thirty seconds. That's more attainable. When you can do that, set a new lower goal.

Same goes if you're trying to lose fifty pounds. That's a big number! Instead, your goal should be five pounds. If you're losing one pound a week (which should be your goal anyway), you can hit that goal in about a month! Then you just set a new goal: five more pounds. You keep doing that until you get to those fifty pounds.

I used to weigh more than 300 pounds. I currently weigh 220. My goal was to get to around 200, which was (and is) quite a daunting task. Instead, I first made my goal 280. Then 270. Then 260. I kept at it. Right now, my current goal is 210. Smaller goals help you get to the larger ones.

> *Smaller goals help you get to the larger ones.*

WEIGH YOURSELF DAILY!

If you're trying to lose weight, or gain weight, or just stay where you are, weighing yourself daily, at about the same time, and averaging the results, is a good way to stay accountable. Your weight fluctuates a lot. If you only weighed yourself once a week, so many factors come into play that could affect how much you weigh.

If you had some salty food the day before, you'll store extra water weight. If you haven't pooped for a while, same thing. If you're dehydrated, or if you ate foods that literally didn't weigh as much, same thing.

SLEEP MORE!

Your body needs at least eight hours every night to repair the damage you've done to it just by existing. If you're exercising regularly, it may need even more sleep. The more time you're catching winks, the more time it has to fix everything.

More sleep works toward keeping you healthier in mind and body, which keeps you well rested and able to make better decisions, all of which pushes you closer to whatever your health goals are. Hell yeah. Sleep!

So in conclusion: Eat less (or more, as needed). Move more. Drink more water. Sleep more. Eat more protein, less bad carbs. Weigh yourself daily. Change your weight slowly. You got this.

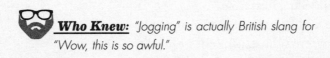

Who Knew: *"Jogging" is actually British slang for "Wow, this is so awful."*

You Won't Ever Look like That Celebrity and That's Okay

I USED TO HATE THE FACT THAT I DIDN'T LOOK LIKE BRAD PITT IN *Fight Club.* Go check online to see what I'm talking about. I'll wait.

See? I mean, damn, look at those *abs.* And his biceps and triceps? Dude looks cut as hell. And his spiky hair? Totally baller. That was how I wanted to look when I was in high school. Except there's only one problem.

I'll never look like Brad Pitt. I'll never look like any famous and sexy celebrity. From a Kardashian butt to a Chris Hemsworth pectoral, we're shown these great specimens of genetics (and sometimes plastic surgery!) and told *that* is what beauty is. We should look like them. Or else we've failed.

I'm here to tell you to never feel bad for not looking like these people. How they look is unattainable for the average person for a whole slew of reasons.

THEY HAVE A WHOLE TEAM TO MAKE THEM LOOK BEAUTIFUL

From trainers to chefs to makeup artists to clothing designers, the people you see gracing the covers of magazines have a gaggle of paid talent to make them look amazing. Most of us are lucky to have friends who can tell us whether or not our shirts match our pants.

It's like thinking, after watching Tom Brady, that you're bad at throwing a football. He has hundreds of people around to help make him amazing at throwing footballs. (He also manages to make UGG boots look great. What skill!) So why feel bad when you don't look like a glamorous celebrity?

THEY DON'T EAT LIKE MOST PEOPLE DO

Part of a celebrity's job is to look beautiful always. Because of that, eating healthy becomes part of celebrities' job. So much so, that many hire chefs to cook them expensive meals. Their entire diet is perfectly figured out by someone whose job it is to make them look gorgeous. The average person doesn't have access to that, so don't sweat it.

THEY HAVE MORE TIME TO GO TO THE GYM THAN WE DO

The Rock goes to the gym six days a week, for at least ninety minutes a day. Oh, and he runs a lot. He also has decades of experience working out in the gym. So why should you feel bad for not having quads as big as his? Don't. (Hi, Dwayne! You're awesome.) Most people's jobs don't require them to look like hulking muscle monsters, so they don't give you time to get that kind of body. That's okay.

THEY ONLY LOOK THAT WAY FOR MOMENTS AT A TIME

Here's the secret they don't tell you about the people on the covers of fitness magazines: They have worked for months to lead up to a thirty-minute window for taking those photos. They bulked up then starved their body of food and water for weeks so they would look shredded. Just to look amazing in that photo.

As soon as the shoot is over, they drink water and eat carbohydrates and their body looks more normal. That ripped and shredded look doesn't last forever. It's just a snapshot. So why chase that?

THEIR PHOTOS ARE EDITED BY MAGICIANS

Photos of celebrities get touched up by photo editors to make them look even more amazing than they already do. They're *faked*. Your

Instagram posts don't have a highly trained professional editing out your freckles and making your arms look more toned. So why compare yourself to that? Don't.

THEIR GENETICS ARE NOT YOUR GENETICS

Not everyone's bodies are made to look the same. So why chase how someone else is destined to look because of their inherited genes? You'll never have that. You're meant to look like *you*. And you are pretty great.

Mobility and Stretching, OMG

I DIDN'T STRETCH FOR ABOUT TWENTY-NINE STRAIGHT YEARS. AFTER I started exercising regularly, I began reading about this magical thing where you move your body a little bit in different directions, and it should help you out in wonderful ways. I would stretch my arms, my legs, my back, my neck, all the basics. It didn't seem to make any sense what I was doing, or why I was doing it.

Then one day, about nine months into lifting weights, I was standing in my kitchen and I had a crazy thought. "I've never been able to bend down and touch my toes," I said out loud, giving any nosy neighbors even more of a reason to think I'm weird. "I wonder if I can." If I stretched my legs, I usually did it while on my butt, or while pushing a leg against a wall to stretch my hamstrings. I hadn't actually tried to bend over and touch my toes in a long time.

Mostly because I had this big-ass belly in the way, so it would constrict my breathing. (When I was fatter, just bending to tie my shoes was a chore. I had to hold my breath damn near the entire time. Yeah, I know. Jesus, Andy.)

When bending over, I could barely ever make it past my shins. Touching my toes was like this fable I only heard about in grade school phys ed. The teacher said I should be able to do it. I could even see other kids do it. But me, personally? Hell no.

Then that fateful day in the kitchen, I said, "To hell with it," and bent down. Then I immediately began crying. Because I was easily able to touch my goddamn toes. It was the first time in my entire life I could remember doing it. I had to sit down on the floor because I was overtaken with emotion.

It was one of those happy cries, like when you get married or get to board a plane before everyone else. My cat came over and licked my head, because whenever I am close to ground level it's easier for him to attempt to eat me. As I sobbed, I stood back up, just to make sure I hadn't imagined it.

I leaned forward and did it again. And again. And again. All those months of stretching regularly allowed me to do this dumb thing I hadn't ever been able to do.

Maybe your thing isn't touching your toes. Maybe your thing is to run a mile, or be able to hold your breath for a minute and not feel like you're going to die. Maybe you'd like to have sex against a wall. (You do. Trust me. [Sorry, Mom.]) Either way, taking better care of yourself, especially when it comes to mobility, goes a long way toward making these things possible. Did I mention the wall thing?

Sure, for me, the weight loss also helped. So did a few leg exercises I did in the gym, which helped stretch the muscles and allowed me to bend further. But holy shit, the toe-touching thing? Amazing.

So now I have a new goal. I want to be able to do the splits. I'm coming for you, Jean-Claude Van Damme. Watch the fuck out, bro.

> **_Pro Tip:_** Lower back pain is sometimes caused by tight hamstrings and glutes. So one way to alleviate the pain is to stop being such a tightass.

More about Your Body and Self-Doubt!

I TOLD MYSELF IF I JUST GOT IN BETTER SHAPE, THAT'D FIX ALL THE problems in my brain. All that doubt and self-hatred would wash away, draining out of me like sweat on a bench. I would be always happy, always carefree, and never have to worry about anything again.

Turns out that was wrong.

I still get supersad sometimes. I'll get in a depressive funk that won't go away. My brain will steer me toward self-destruction. It sucks. A lot.

I thought if I made myself more visually appealing, if I became objectively more attractive to the world, it would mean more people would like me and love me.

I thought that would somehow fill that emptiness inside of me, the void that's been present since I ever could remember, ever since kids called me fat. Ever since I couldn't find clothes because I was too large. Ever since almost the entirety of society told me I should be ashamed of myself because of what I'd let happen to my body.

That's not the case at all. If anything, the nothingness is bigger now. Because I look at myself in the mirror, and I know all the progress I've made, but I can still grab at my stomach and call myself fat. As I type this, I'm skinnier than I was in high school. I was just a normal-sized kid back then, even, but everyone else in my memory was bone thin.

Quick story: We used to play shirts versus skins in PE class when I was younger. I don't know what evil fucker thought it would be cool to tell middle schoolers to take their shirts off, but whoever it was should burn in hell. But I was so large, kids would always force me to play on team shirts because no one wanted to see me shirtless. I wasn't *that* fat, but, man, that's always stuck with me.

What I'm trying to say is, fuck middle school.

By comparison, I was huge. So I was made to hate my body. Not to mention, the people on every television show, every movie, every famous rock star and misguided idol I had growing up, they were all devilishly good-looking. And thin. That was what I wanted, not knowing that many people achieve those bodies through either crazy genetics or steroids on top of intense workout schedules.

That hatred of myself and my body, fueled by constant bullying throughout my life because of my size, that just doesn't go away because I can fit into normal-sized pants. I still see a fat kid in the mirror. One who isn't worthy of anyone's love.

I know I've destroyed relationships and friendships because of that self-hatred. It told me that anyone who was dumb enough to love this ugly sack of shit was an idiot, so I needed to pick at them until whatever they liked about me was beaten out of them. I would ignore people, I would belittle them, I would attack, just to make them realize how *stupid* they were for wanting to care about someone like me.

But that's total bullshit. I do deserve to be loved, regardless of how I look. So do you. Everyone does. No matter what. Always and forever. We're all beautiful creatures, made to look different on purpose. I'm lucky that I was able to get into a mind-set that allowed me to push myself toward success when it came to fitness.

I know that not everyone is. I also know that a hundred years ago, my formerly large body would've been seen by most of society as *fine as hell*. The fatter you were, the more opulent your life and thus the more respected you were.

Not to mention, I found plenty of people who cared about me and didn't mind how I looked. One ex-girlfriend, when I talked with her recently about my weight loss, thought when we dated I was normal sized. Now she thinks I'm just skin and bones.

This is normal. Lots of people feel this way about their bodies. But your body is just a part of who you are. What happens in your mind is what's important, and learning to love how you look is an important skill to learn. Because your body will always change. You'll always think something is a little wrong with it. That's just how we're wired.

You *can* change some things about how your body looks. I'm proof. But in spite of my more slender physique, I still have to work on reinforcing a positive self-image.

That's what I do, every day, by looking into a mirror and telling myself I'm awesome. And you should, too.

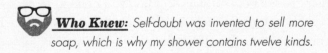

Who Knew: *Self-doubt was invented to sell more soap, which is why my shower contains twelve kinds.*

The Art of Relaxing

I WAS NEVER GOOD AT RELAXING. EVEN WHEN I WAS YOUNGER, I AL- ways had to be doing *something*. It wasn't until I was in my late twenties that I figured out it wasn't that I was bad at relaxing, but rather that I disliked what most people thought was relaxing. So here are my favorite ways to relax.

1. Going for a walk. Not only is it light exercise, but it allows me to explore wherever I am and discover new things. I usually listen to a podcast or an audiobook and just aimlessly wander around whatever town I'm in (always after making sure I know which neighborhoods aren't safe to walk through).

2. Driving aimlessly. Whenever I have access to a car, I like to just drive around. Similar to when I walk without a plan, that's what I do with a car. For me, it's never about knowing where I'm going. It's about discovering new parts of the city I'm in, seeing what's around, letting my mind be free and do whatever it wants.

3. Sitting on a bench. I could sit on a bench at a park and watch people all day. Just leaning back, listening to the world around me, not thinking about anything in particular. On most weekends, I like to find a new park and just sit and watch people for a while. It's nice to enjoy humanity and watch others have fun. It connects you more with your community and reminds you that we're all in this together.

4. Taking a long shower. I like taking an occasional extralong shower. It's not the best use of water, sure, and can be a bit wasteful, so I'm always mindful of that. But for me, a long shower means a ten-minute shower, because usually I'm only in there for five minutes, tops. (One of the perks of going bald is you don't have to do any fancy shampooing.)

5. Having a massage. Because I lift weights a lot, I regularly need massages to get the knots out of my body, mostly on my back. It generally hurts like hell. But afterward, I feel refreshed. Somehow the pain is relaxing to me. Probably because in the corners of my mind, it *seems* like work, because it's making my body better.

6. Calling my parents. Talking to my mom or dad on the phone is always a nice way for me to relax. Shooting the shit with anyone is great, but for me my parents are always a nice respite from my daily life. I get to hear about their world, and clue them in on what I'm doing lately, and it almost always includes lots of laughing.

7. Reading. Sometimes reading feels like work for me. I'm analyzing how the writer's doing such a damn good job telling a story. But when I can get out of my way and let my brain go and explore this world that's been invented for me, that's when I can truly relax. Hours will pass and I won't even know it. That's the best.

8. Playing with a pet. Even though he sometimes poops in my bathtub, it's lots of fun to just run around my place with a string and watch my cat run after me. He gets supercompetitive, trying to destroy whatever toy I'm teasing him with. He's also relatively okay just sleeping on my shoulders on the back of the couch while I'm just sitting there.

9. Playing video games. I'm new to this world. As in, just a few weeks ago, my doctor told me I needed to learn to relax better, and she suggested playing video games. I hadn't touched them in ten years, but *holy crap*. They're all basically amazing movies, except you get to play inside of them! Not only do you get to escape to another world, but you get to hear fascinating stories told by amazing writers. And you get to jump and solve puzzles and feel fantastic afterward. Just remember to come back to reality every once in a while, as video games can become addictive.

Pro Tip: The first book that popularized the idea of relaxing was published in 1929, just in time for the Great Depression!

Get a Damn Bedtime

MOST OF US AREN'T GETTING ENOUGH SLEEP. YOU PROBABLY AREN'T, either. Sleep is not just a time for your body to rest and repair itself. It's also when your brain defragments itself and works out problems in your life.

If you're never sleeping, not only will you be physically tired, but your brain can't do its important work, either. Your bed should be used for only two things: sleeping and sex. (Congrats on getting the latter!)

Here are some other tips to help you get the best night's sleep possible:

1. Set a bedtime. It may take some experimenting, but you'll want to go to bed early enough that you don't need to wake up with an alarm clock in the morning. An alarm clock should be more of a backup measure, just in case you accidentally sleep in. If you have trouble waking up in the morning, it's usually because you're not going to sleep early enough.

You should go to bed early enough so your body gets the sleep it needs, then wakes you up. For me, that bedtime is eleven p.m., which is what allows me to wake up before eight a.m.

2. Set bed expectations. Your body needs to know that when you lie down in your bed it's time to fall asleep. So you may need to retrain yourself from our modern lifestyle of having screens around us at all times. Your bedroom shouldn't have a television, a tablet, or anything else that emits a light while you're trying to go to sleep.

Same goes for other distractions: If you like to read before bed, do it on the couch. If you want to watch late-night television, do it in the living room. Make it so whenever you lie down, your brain thinks, "Ah, it's bedtime, and I am now in bed. Zzzzzz." Start changing your habits in the bedroom and that will help.

3. Keep your bedroom dark. You should try to keep where you sleep as dark as possible, as this helps your body think it's sleep time. The more lights (especially from the screens of devices) you can see, the harder it is to sleep, because it can impact your circadian rhythm.

Try wearing a sleep mask. They work. I used one when I lived in a house where the sun blasted into my bedroom hours before I needed to wake up. Wearing it made it seem as if the sun never rose. (Which also sounds like the title to a terrible Hemingway sequel.)

4. If you can't sleep, get up for ten minutes. Go do something that requires your brain and your hands, such as reading a book, doing a puzzle, cleaning your kitchen.

You want to make sure you don't associate your bed with being awake, so if you can't fall asleep, go do something else for a while. Then when you head back to bed, your brain switches itself into thinking, "Oh, yeah, that's where I go to sleep!"

5. Don't keep a visible alarm clock. Moving the digital alarm clock out of my bedroom immensely helped me sleep. Constantly checking it when I couldn't sleep made me calculate how few hours of sleep I'd be getting. That made me more stressed, which prevented me from sleeping.

Now if I wake up in the middle of the night, I have no clue what time it is, or how many hours until I'm supposed to be awake. So I fall right back asleep much easier.

6. Keep your room cold. The sweatier you are, the harder it is to sleep. I try to keep my room pretty chilled—around 69 degrees (lol 69) if possible—throughout the year.

Your body temperature dips slightly when you're falling asleep. So if you keep your room cooler, it can help speed up the process of you catching some z's.

7. Exercise. I've never slept better than when I started walking at least five miles a day and began regularly lifting weights. By the time bedtime rolls around, my body is aching to hit the sheets. It needs to rest and rebuild the muscles I've pounded throughout the day.

By adding some more vigorous movement throughout your day, you'll tire your body out, so it'll want to fall asleep as soon as it's able.

EXTRA LIFE SLEEP TIP EXTRAVAGANZA: *Before you go to bed, think for a few minutes about any big problems you're working on, either at work, in your life, or anything. Your brain's subconscious is always working in the background, especially while you sleep. If you go to bed actively thinking about something you need to solve, when you wake up, your brain sometimes has the answer. It's worked for me and many others. Hopefully it'll work for you, too.*

> **Hot Take:** Guinness World Records *says the largest bed is eighty-six feet, eleven inches long and fifty-three feet, eleven inches wide, which still isn't big enough to hold Kanye West's ego.*

Get a Damn Dentist

WHEN YOU'RE IN YOUR MIDTWENTIES, YOU TRULY BELIEVE YOU'RE indestructible. You kind of are. You can drink for an entire night and then go to work and feel relatively okay. (Did that.) You can jump off a house at a party and land in a bush (did that, too) and barely have any scrapes. But one area you should not fuck with is your goddamn teeth.

I found this out the relatively hard way as I was fixing all the various parts of my life. After I got my diet and exercise in check, I realized my mouth wasn't feeling so great. I brushed my teeth once—sometimes even *twice!*—every day. Flossing was a joke, because everyone knows you only floss in those two weeks before your next dental appointment. Problem was, I hadn't been to a dentist in years. So I hadn't flossed in forever.

One morning, after brushing my teeth, I stared in the mirror and was about to say nice things about myself. Then I smiled. Then I freaked out.

My teeth were covered in blood.

I didn't know what the hell was happening, so I immediately searched on "teeth covered in blood." The results were drastic: I *definitely* had mouth cancer. At the very least, I would lose all my teeth and be forced to get gum transplants from dead people. (Yes, that's a thing.) I hadn't been to a dentist in years, so I didn't know what to do.

Fortunately, I had dental insurance. Using my insurance's terrible website, I found local dentists who would take my insurance. The first two were superbusy and didn't seem to care about my pain and could get me in as early as 2071. The third dentist I called, not only was he right down the street, but he could see me the next morning. My mouth almost started to feel better already.

At the appointment, he introduced himself and told me about how his office worked. He wasn't as concerned with fixing cosmetic issues right away, he told me. The health of my mouth was the most important, so we would work on that. Then after a quick exam of my mouth, he was, like, "So, you haven't been to a dentist in a while, have you?" He knew. They always know.

I had severe gingivitis, partially because I wasn't flossing, I wasn't brushing my teeth right (Did you know you can do it *wrong*? Because you can!), and I hadn't had a cleaning in forever. He ordered a deep clean, which could do only half of my mouth at a time because it was, as he put it, mildly unpleasant. My dentist also counted many cavities, all of which needed immediate help. And on top of that, he said my fillings needed to be replaced. Had I been to a dentist in recent years, they would've taken out my old ones, which used outdated materials that *apparently* can cause cancer. (My Googling was on point!)

The next two weeks was a blur of dental appointments. My dentist prescribed me this industrial-strength mouthwash, which tasted like an abandoned car factory in Detroit. I would almost hurl after every use. Then I had two of those "deep-cleaning" experiences, which involved a dental hygienist apologizing profusely before giving me enough pain to make me realize how important flossing is. When I was healed from that, my dentist then started on fixing my cavities and replacing my fillings. I left most of our sessions with a back caked in sweat, a numb mouth, and an internalized sense of the importance of dental health.

So you need to get a goddamn dentist. You need to floss your teeth every day, like I do now. You also need to brush your teeth twice a day, preferably with an electric toothbrush. If you wanna go nuts and use mouthwash, go right ahead, but hopefully yours isn't prescription strength like mine.

I would call it an inconvenient truth (I almost made a joke about an inconvenient tooth here, but c'mon, I'm above that), but in reality it's not even that inconvenient. Dental hygiene takes only a few minutes a day. It can save you a world of pain and money down the line.

> **_Pro Tip:_** *If you try to schedule an appointment with your dentist at "tooth hurty," they hang up.*

One Weird Trick to Look Cool without Giving Yourself Cancer

DON'T SMOKE. THE ONLY REASON YOU DO IT IS TO LOOK COOL. YOU know what else looks cool? Wearing a leather jacket.

Not to mention, it's way cheaper. Here in Chicago, a pack of cigarettes is about twelve dollars. If you smoke a pack a day, that's almost $4,400 a year. You know how much a good leather jacket costs?

Like, a hundred dollars at a thrift store. Here are more reasons leather jackets are better than smoking:

- They don't give you lung cancer
- If you get in a motorcycle accident, a leather jacket will protect you more than a cigarette
- Your breath won't smell worse while wearing a leather jacket
- It's legal to buy leather jackets for your nephew
- Your leather jacket can't accidentally set your apartment on fire

Don't vape, either. It's like smoking, except you don't look cool at all. It's like the opposite of wearing a leather jacket.

> **Who Knew:** Vaping was invented to answer the question "How do I let everyone know they shouldn't have sex with me?"

NEXT-LEVEL
Awesomeness

Failing Isn't Failure

THE ONLY REASON I'M AT ALL GOOD AT ANYTHING IS BECAUSE I'VE
failed at it a lot. I've made mistakes, I've learned from those mistakes, and thus I've acquired skills in that area. That's it.

So when you fail, it's not a total failure, because you usually learn from it. Every huge professional bungle I've had in my life (and—ha ha ha—I've had a lot), they've all taught me something. Usually what they schooled me on was that I needed to fail more. As long as you're learning from your mistakes, failing isn't failure.

The problem with most things is we only see the finished product. You're not reading the first version of this book. I wrote a rough draft, then I edited it. Then I edited it again. Then again. Then I had friends give me notes. Then my agent. Then my editor. Then some copy editors. Then probably my mom, who I hope skips the sections about sex. Then me some more. And now you.

You see the end result, not all the attempts before. When you watch someone shred on the guitar, you're not seeing the hours of rehearsal beforehand. When you see an amazing painting, you don't see the ten others the artist threw away because they turned out wrong. You don't see the mistakes. So don't be lied to. Because failing is how we all make better shit.

IT'S OKAY FOR OTHERS TO SUCCEED

When someone else succeeds, it doesn't diminish your own success. Just because someone else gets something you want, it doesn't mean you missed out

Never view someone else's success as your failure.

on it. It just means that other person did something cool. It's not as if they *took* something from you. So never view someone else's success as your failure. Because it's not.

No one knows everything. Everyone fucks up and that's okay. It's what gets you closer to greatness.

> **Hot Take:** *My single greatest failure is not becoming an astronaut. Second place: I once had a goatee.*

Life Isn't Fair and That Sucks

MY FIRST MEMORY OF REJECTION WAS ASKING MY PARENTS FOR some dumb toy at the store. Whatever the toy was doesn't matter. I probably would've gotten it, played with it for ten minutes, gotten bored, and found a way to break it in a fantastically cute way or barter it with a neighborhood kid for some other hand-me-down. I just remember the "no" from my parents. I cried and said, "It isn't fair!" And one of my parents just smiled, ignoring my incessant cries of pain and anguish, then said, "Life isn't fair."

I was angry at them for days. But they were right. And once I finally internalized that life isn't fair, it was easier to deal with everything. Some people are born rich. Some people are born without their right arms. Some people learn to slam dunk behind their backs. Others can't even afford food. It sucks. Because the world isn't fair, that means many things are out of your control. So what should you do when faced with a world that isn't actually a meritocracy?

Focus on what you *can* control. That means yourself and your actions. When something doesn't go your way, keep your head high and continue working. Because you know the world isn't tilted toward your favor. Because life isn't fair. But you *can* control how you respond to the world not being fair, by continuing to bust your ass and stay positive.

One of my favorite examples is about a guy who was a struggling writer, barely making ends meet. He grew up submitting short stories to magazines, routinely getting rejected. He kept writing, though, eventually graduating college with an English degree. Married and with a family to support, he got a teaching job. He kept writing. He kept getting rejections.

Eventually, he wrote a novel and sent it out. It was rejected thirty times. Finally, his book got noticed. It was published, albeit with a relatively small advance of $2,500. Sales picked up speed and the paperback rights were sold for $400,000.

The book was *Carrie* by Stephen King. You *may* have heard of him. You're probably scared of clowns because of him. (I know I am.) But if there's anyone out there who personifies the idea of just continuing to do the work despite the world not being fair, it's him.

Side note: J. K. Rowling, the author of the *Harry Potter* series (did I seriously have to tell you that?), had the first book about our bespectacled friend rejected about a dozen times before it was accepted. The editor who accepted it told her she shouldn't quit her day job. That book alone has since sold more than 100 million copies.

So whenever you're sad that something doesn't go your way, just remember you can control only one thing: yourself. If you keep working hard and pushing yourself, despite life not being fair, you'll eventually find success.

It may not be necessarily the success you were striving toward. But you will, at the least, become more accomplished at whatever it is you're working on. Sometimes that's the best reward you can get.

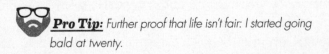 ***Pro Tip:*** *Further proof that life isn't fair: I started going bald at twenty.*

Nobody Knows Anything

I WAS TWENTY-FOUR WHEN I REALIZED NOBODY KNOWS ANYTHING.
I was a newbie reporter at Florida's biggest newspaper. One afternoon we were all assembled outside of the top editor's office. We were wearing paper cutouts of his face, blasting the University of Iowa fight song, and he was running past us, high-fiving us all.

The University of Iowa had just inducted him into its hall of fame for being an overall badass. We were doing this little ceremony because we were proud of our top boss man and his accomplishments. Something fun, something silly. After he ran down the line, another editor read off his list of life achievements. That was when it all hit me like a barrel of bowling balls.

The top editor worked at his college newspaper, just like me. This guy interned at other newspapers, just like me. He went to a big dumb state school, just like me. So, just like me, this guy has no clue what he's doing. We're all faking our way through life, making decisions based on past experiences.

If this giant of journalism, who oversees the biggest newspaper in Florida and hundreds of people, doesn't know anything, then nobody else knows anything. Holy shit. My mind kept expanding on that idea: Airplane pilots don't know what they're doing, but they can still fly planes. Doctors don't know if a treatment will actually help you, but often it does. Dancers don't know whether their dance moves are perfect, but they can still amaze you with their talent.

As I stood there, half listening to the editor's short speech about what we had done for him, life suddenly became a lot easier. We're all just making this up as we go. We make mistakes and then we learn from them. Then we make more mistakes and we learn from those. Repeat repeat repeat.

Never feel bad if you don't know something. Because nobody knows anything. We're all just faking this, some of us with more mistakes than others. You'll soon have a lot more mistakes to learn from, too. Maybe someday you'll get to high-five a bunch of underlings while they wear cutouts of your face. If not, think deeply to yourself where your life went wrong and try to fix it.

Don't Get a Pet Tarantula

YOU KNOW WHO ELSE HAD BUGS AS PETS? BUFFALO BILL IN *SILENCE* *of the Lambs*. Don't be like Buffalo Bill. Get a dog or a cat. If you're into steampunk, only then can you get a lizard.

Good Lord, Don't Wear Blackface

RACISM IS REAL AND IT EXISTS. IF YOU'RE WHITE AND SAYING "NO, it doesn't!" maybe go talk to someone who isn't white. I'll wait.

Yeah, see? Holy shit, pretty awful, right? Because you're reading this book, you're obviously trying to improve yourself. So I thought I'd make a list of things white people can't do.

You may say, "But Andy! I'm just having fun!" Sure! But your having fun can also be *totally racist*. Is your having fun so important that it's worth making someone else feel awful?

If your answer to that is yes, go back and read the Asshole Test chapter twenty-seven more times.

Here's a not complete list of things white people can't do. I'm not going to explain any of them. Just trust me on this, okay? Like many people, I've done racist things and said racist shit because I was ignorant, or worse, because I didn't care. You should work at making yourself less ignorant and learn to empathize with those who are different than you. If I can work on diminishing the prejudices I was raised with, anyone can. This list is a good start.

Do not:

- Dress in blackface
- Say the n-word
- Wear a sombrero
- Say the word "coon"
- Say "Hitler had some good ideas"

- Use Martin Luther King Jr.'s rhetoric to defend doing something that would make MLK, if he knew about it, be, like, "WTF?"
- Tell people to pull themselves up by their bootstraps
- Define an entire race or religion by something one person did
- Try to hook up two people you know just because they happen to be the same race
- Point out the race of someone when telling a story when it has nothing to do with anything at all
- Ask someone, "But where are you *really* from?"
- Say you don't date someone of a certain race because you're not "into" that
- Only date someone of a certain race because you're "into" that
- Pretend it's okay for you to say racist jokes because you have one black friend
- Say racist jokes
- Ever say "my one black friend"
- Say "if they just work hard they'll get ahead"
- Say the success of [insert the name of a nonwhite celebrity] proves racism is over
- Say you "don't see color" (lol)
- Say you can relate to the racism that a person of color felt because of some "similar situation" you encountered
- Require a person of color to speak for their entire race
- Give Macklemore a Grammy

Why I Don't Worry So Much Anymore

FOR MANY THINGS IN YOUR LIFE, YOU HAVE TWO POSSIBLE OUT- comes: yes or no.

As an example, let's say you've interviewed for a job. You think it went well. Now you're just waiting to hear back from them. Either you get the job or you don't. It's a yes or a no.

When I was younger, I used to fret about the possibility of not getting the job. It meant I was a total failure, a fraud, just the worst. Sure, I already had a job, but ugh, if I didn't get that new one, I would be ruined!

But now I know something even more important: If I don't get that job, it's not a negative. It's neutral. Sure, not getting the job kind of sucks, but it's not like my life changes. I still have a job. The absence of a good thing isn't a *negative* thing. It just is.

So what's the point in worrying about something neutral happening? It's a waste of your brain time. More importantly, it's gonna make you feel anxious and awful. Because either you get the job (hooray!) or you don't (oh, well, no worries).

In almost every one of these options in life, either something good happens or nothing happens. As far as I'm concerned, it's a win-win scenario, like ordering a pizza and tacos and instead they deliver taco pizza.

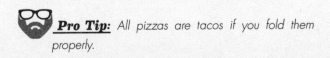 **Pro Tip:** *All pizzas are tacos if you fold them properly.*

How to Get Good at Damn Near Anything

WHEN I WAS IN COLLEGE, I USED TO TELL PEOPLE I WAS A WRITER. I read a lot *about* writing. I read a lot of books. I thought all the time about what would make a great story, a great hook. I was doing everything a writer should be doing.

Except writing.

The main way you get better at anything is by doing that thing over and over and over. Sounds simple, but my life is proof that it works. (Most lives are, actually.) As is the fact that we have seen billions of people throughout history who have gotten good at shit.

To paraphrase a Macklemore lyric (because quoting it would literally require me to ask him permission to include it in a book) that's always stuck with me: The greatest painters weren't great because they could paint awesome at birth. They became great because they practiced their craft frequently.

So that's what you should do if you plan on getting good at damn near anything. Other than that, here are some other hints.

■ **Surround yourself with people better than you.** When I was starting out as a comedian, I was lucky enough to do it in Boston, a city with a strong comedy community. Every day of the week I could see people doing what I wanted to do at a high level.

Every show at the Improv Asylum, an improv theater in the city's North End, was like a master class in being hilarious. Same thing for most of the stand-up comedy shows.

I immersed myself in that world, just making sure I could be around people who were better than me at comedy. Eventually, just by watching them do what they do, you learn a few tricks. It's the only time trickle-down economics ever works.

■ **Take classes.** Not everyone is able to surround themselves with people more skilled than themselves. But odds are, someone's teaching a class in a skill you want to get better at. Just Google your city's name and the thing you want to get better at. If I look up "Chicago cooking classes" oh, my God, I get so many options. Did you know couples take cooking classes? Wow, what a world we live in.

Classes are great because they're usually taught by an expert, or someone who at the very least knows more than you. It'll also help you get surrounded with other people who may be at your level, or a little more ahead. This lets you find a local community of people who are also interested in the thing you enjoy.

■ **Know you're gonna suck.** What you don't often learn about getting good at shit is, well, you are usually awful when you start out. You know you're awful because you like cool shit.

When I was learning guitar, I loved all these shred metal gods, these people who were the fastest guitar players of all time. So here I thought I was the worst, because I was comparing myself to *literally the greatest guitarists ever.*

That's like being a Little League first baseman and being pissed you're not as good as [insert famous first baseman here, or maybe don't, because it's funnier if you intentionally leave this blank— yeah, I'm gonna leave it blank]. See how ridiculous that seems? Your taste is so much better than your talent, so you know how big the gap is.

You should compare yourself with only yourself.

This is why you should compare yourself with only yourself. You aren't competing against anyone else. If you're a writer, you're not trying to be better than Joan Didion. (Because you're just not gonna be, okay?) You're trying to be better than you were six months ago.

That's why you should be *always doing the thing you want to get better at.*

Because after six months, go back and look at your old work. You'll go, "Wow, I'm not as bad as I used to be! Holy shit, I am getting better!" You will still think you suck, because your tastes are *always* ahead of your talents. But you can at least appreciate that you have, objectively, gotten better than you once were.

That's what's important. Knowing that even though you kind of always think you suck, after some time you don't suck as much. I cringe when I go back and watch videos of me doing stand-up comedy five years ago. It's so so so so so so so so bad. It's so cliché. I don't even know how to stand on stage and breathe.

But if I watch a recent clip, I can tell I'm better than that older version of me. There's still a lot I'm not happy with, but it's better.

■ **Set goals for yourself.** I already talked about this at length in a previous chapter ("Measure Success by Setting Goals"), but it's important enough to mention again. Make them quantifiable. By that, I mean something you can measure. If you're into cooking, your goal can be "try three new dishes a week." If you're into writing, it could be "write one thousand words a day." If you're trying to get better at painting, it can be "paint for sixty minutes each day." You can set up a spreadsheet, or a calendar, to track yourself.

■ **It's okay to decide you don't wanna do something anymore.** I played guitar for hours every day from sixth grade through the end of high school. I joined bands. I played shows whenever I could. I recorded albums in my basement. But then I reached a point where I just didn't want to play guitar anymore, so I kind of just stopped.

That's totally fine. You can get to a level of ability you're happy with and you don't need to push yourself further. It's not *bad* if you want to do something just as a hobby, even if others want to make you feel that way because you're not dedicating your life to something. (Ever know someone's mom or dad who jammed with a cover band on the weekend? I'm going to be that guy someday. I can't wait.)

Sometimes it feels good to take a guitar out, plug it into an amp, turn it up loud, and blast out some chords. Doesn't mean everyone needs to end up joining Coldplay. (A note to any members of Coldplay reading this: First of all, thanks for making music that me *and* my mom can both enjoy. And secondly, "Fix You" made me cry at a Walgreens once. Thanks!)

How to Be Confident in
Any Situation

I TRY TO ACT LIKE I KNOW WHAT I'M DOING IN ALMOST ANY SITUA-
tion. It's worked pretty well for most of my life. I've blustered my
way through countless meetings, scared out of my mind, unsure of
anything I was saying, by just telling myself, "You're doing great,
keep going."

Because everyone else is also kind of faking what they're doing.
None of us *really* knows what we're doing. If you're confident,
though, not only does it make you
sound like you know what you're talking about, you'll actually *think* you're
not completely full of shit. (Also, to
check my privilege here, being a white
man has definitely helped me in many
situations where I was talking out of

> *None of us* really *knows*
> *what we're doing.*

my ass, regardless of my actual skill.) If you sound like you know,
and you think you know, what you're doing, other people will think
you do, too. It's the magic sauce in a tasty confidence sandwich.
(Mmm ... sandwiches.)

Another few tips before you're about to give a talk or go on a
date or do anything that gives you the willies:

■ **Visualize your success.** Before whatever you're about to do
that's stressful, think about how it'll go awesomely. Visualize the
best possible outcome, and how you'll make it a success and be incredible. Tell yourself, "This is how it's going to go down." And repeat that it *is* going to be a success, no matter what.

■ **Stand like Superman.** While you're visualizing your success, stand like Superman (or Wonder Woman!) for five minutes. Or sit in a chair and make yourself big and open. This is called a "high-power" pose. It changes hormone levels in your body, if the science can be believed, lowering your cortisol, for instance, which can give you more concentration and confidence. When you sit scrunched up, in a "low-power" pose, it makes you feel weak. But when you make yourself big, your brain views itself as stronger and superior, and then you act accordingly. Even if this science is all junk, it's worked for me and my friends countless times, so maybe it just helps to calm one's brain and get you in the right mind-set for success. If you're worried about someone judging you for doing this, do it in a bathroom stall. Or, better yet, don't give a shit because, screw them, you're doing your damnedest to be a success and that's awesome. (I know, this sounds like bullshit, but trust me, it works.)

■ **Smile.** I always try to smile whenever I'm feeling freaked out. It helps to calm me down. Not only that, it makes me look like I know what the fuck I'm doing when I totally do not. At the very least, people looking at you will think you're being pleasant. So they'll think happy thoughts about you, as opposed to if you were grimacing or looking pissed the entire time. This is especially important for those of us who have resting pissy face. (No, I'm not calling it resting bitch face, because that's sexist. Stop being sexist, please.)

■ **Slow down.** When nervous, many people have the tendency to speak superfast, almost as if their mouths are auditioning to be stunt drivers for *The Fast and the Furious* franchise. You need to tell yourself to slow down whenever you're in a stressful situation. Your words become more powerful if you speak slower, too. It gives people more time to digest what you're saying. Not only that, it gives *you* more time to think about what you're saying, allowing you to sound like a confident badass. Win-win.

■ **Keep your body open.** Don't cross your arms. Don't scrunch into a ball. If you're standing, keep your head high and chest forward. Same as standing like Superman, keeping yourself in a "high-power" pose throughout stressful situations makes you seem more confident to others than you may actually feel.

■ **Tell yourself you're doing great.** If self-doubt creeps into your brain, just take a second and reinforce to yourself that you're doing fantastic. Just say to yourself, "You're killing it!" Because you probably are, you badass son of a bitch. Keep going.

No matter how these stressful situations go down, once they're done they're done. You always learn from them, so even if they don't go your way, they're still a success. Sure, it could've gone a different way, and you could've gotten a better outcome. But what matters most is you telling yourself that no matter what happens, you're better for having the experience. Because you truly are.

> **_Hot Take:_** Instead of picturing your audience naked, imagine everyone's wearing a "Who Farted?" T-shirt.

How to Save Your Damn Money

WHEN I WAS YOUNGER I PLAYED LOTS OF ROLE-PLAYING VIDEO games. I'd be some character on a quest, fighting monsters, gaining gold coins, saving the kingdom. Occasionally I'd want to buy some new weapons. If a sword cost a thousand gold coins, but I had only five hundred, I couldn't buy it.

Instead, I used the lesser sword I had for a while, until I saved up enough money for my fancy sword. Then, before I actually bought it, I thought long and hard: Do I really need this sword? What about some tents? Should I perhaps buy some armor instead? If I still thought the sword was worth it, I would buy it.

That video game logic is how I still deal with my finances today. I don't buy things unless I have the money for them. And when I do buy them, I wait an extra bit, making sure I *really* want them. That's what you should do, too.

■ **Put money regularly into your savings account.** You should always be putting a certain amount of every paycheck into your savings. It depends on how much you're making and how big your expenses are. But at the very least, try to put twenty-five dollars each paycheck into your savings.

Your savings account also isn't a piggy bank, where you put money only to use it later for frivolous things. It's meant for big purchases or for emergencies. My most recent purchase using my savings account was the down payment for a condo. Before that, I used money from my savings to help me move to Chicago. (And since initially writing this paragraph, my savings account was

used for a new furnace and air conditioner. HA HA HA homeown-
ership.)

I never use my savings to buy a new electronic gadget or to fund
my dream vacation. You can also save up money, separately, in
your checking account, just by not spending as much money in your
day-to-day living. *That's* the money I use for toys. It's called an ex-
pendable income, and your goal is to spend so little money on ne-
cessities that you have some left over to use for fun purchases.

■ **Lower your expenses.** My parents taught me a simple rule: Spend
less than you make. If you're spending more than you're making,
lower your expenses. That may mean cutting back on drinks out
with friends. Or bring your own lunch to work. Instead of going on a
fancy expensive vacation in Mexico with your honey, choose a place
a few hours' drive from home to save money. (I can rhyme!)

Write down how much money you spend on rent, food, utilities,
and everything else. Then subtract all that from your take-home
pay. You should have some money left over. If not, you're underesti-
mating where you're spending your money.

Lots of online services, which you connect your bank account
to, can automatically show how you're spending your money if you
use a debit card or automated payments. Sometimes little things
here and there add up. If you're getting a Starbucks coffee every
day, that's about thirty dollars a week, or $120 a month, that you're
spending on something you could make at home.

If you can afford something, you can buy it. If you can't, start
cutting out those extras, and watching how you spend money, until
you can. And even if you can, think through if you really need it,
because you could always save that money instead.

■ **Don't buy something big unless you have the money.** If you
want that $1,000 television but you've got only $950, you don't buy

it. It's that simple. The only time you should take out a loan at this stage in life is if you're buying a car (and that's also not necessarily the best idea) or if you're buying a home. You generally don't want to take out a loan on depreciable assets. Almost everything, other than property, is going to be a depreciable asset to you. So it doesn't make sense to go into debt to buy it, because in the end that'll just make whatever you want to buy cost more.

So instead, save up for it. If you truly want it, by the time you've saved, either it'll be cheaper or a better, newer version that costs just as much will be out on the market. A win either way for you.

■ **Win the credit card game.** I've had one credit card for the last decade. It's got a buying limit of five hundred dollars, and it was my "emergency card" my parents helped me get more than a decade ago. Just in case I needed a hotel room, a car tow, or a random flight somewhere, I basically had a credit card that could let me do it.

Because of this, I rarely used the card. It didn't have a high enough limit for me to go on a spending spree and fuck myself with debt. It didn't exist as a temptation to make me become beholden to a credit card company. This credit card protected me from myself, but also from credit card companies.

It seems all credit card companies want you to do is get in debt so you're forced to pay them more money over time. Once you're locked in, it's hard to get out. So if you do get a credit card, use it only for purchases you can (and do) always pay off at the end of the month. And it should also be the kind of card that gives you rewards, either frequent-flyer miles or some sort of cashback bonus. Otherwise, the credit card exists to fuck you over and make your life suck more.

■ **Create good credit.** When I was in college, I had the money saved up to buy a new laptop. But my parents instead had me take out a loan with our hometown bank, set up a special checking account with the exact amount of the loan (plus I think the fifty dollars it cost for the loan), and then slowly pay off that loan over the next two years.

I still got the computer, using the money from the bank. But more importantly, I set up proof on paper of me taking out a loan— which I already had the money for, mind you—and paying it off in the background over a few years. This helped increase my credit score, because it showed I was capable of making regular payments on a decent-sized loan.

This made it practically impossible for me to miss a payment. The checking account had all the money I needed. The bank automatically took money from it monthly. It all happened in the background of my life. But when it came time to buy a house, this loan history (and a few other similar short-term loans I'd taken over the years) helped my credit score immensely.

I could've done something similar with a credit card, which also builds up your credit. But this was much less risky. I didn't have any chance of accidentally forgetting to make a payment to the credit card company. In this instance, the bank took care of everything, all for a little fee on top.

> **_Advice:_** You don't have to put your money into big multinational banks, especially if they, say, helped to ruin the economy in the last decade. Credit unions and smaller, local banks are also good options.

Stop Embarrassing Yourself with a Tacky-Looking Home

WHEN YOU'RE GROWING UP, YOUR PARENTS USUALLY GET TO DECIDE how your home is decorated. If your parents were like mine, that usually meant uncomfortable wicker couches (why do these even exist?) and weird porcelain frogs every goddamn where.

But when you hit adulthood, you get to decide how to decorate your home. How you do it will say a lot about yourself. And if you do it poorly, not only can it make your life feel more stressful, it can turn off any potential houseguests.

■ **Put your shit in frames.** The day you leave a dorm room is the day you can no longer hang shit up on your walls with thumbtacks, tape, or putty. If you have a piece of art you love, put it in a frame and hang it up on a nail or something similar.

■ **No more movie posters.** It's amazing you love *Anchorman*. It's not amazing to be in your late twenties and have a poster of it hanging up on your wall (even if it's framed). Unless you literally have a home theater (not just a living room with a big TV), movie posters are kind of, well, icky. Unless you worked on it. Or it *changed your life*. Or whatever. But if it was hanging up in your dorm room, it should probably go.

> *If it was hanging up in your dorm room, it should probably go.*

■ **No black lights.** C'mon, dude.

■ **Have enough plates, glasses, and silverware for eight people.**
I'm thirty and I've never had so many people over that eight plates
weren't enough. Beyond that, you can just use plastic or paper plates
for almost any situation. Think to yourself how many times you've
been superjudgmental because a friend made you eat off paper
plates. Oh, cool, you can't think of a single one? Neither will anyone
ever think that about you. (And if they do, stop inviting them over.)

■ **Have a few wineglasses and tumblers.** If you're of the drinking
sort, have a handful of wineglasses and tumblers for you to be
fancy. It's no longer cool to have all those glasses you stole from the
bar in your cupboard, so get rid of those and buy some decent shit
from Target.

■ **Paper towels.** You should always have paper towels on a roll
somewhere in your kitchen. After I started doing this, my domes-
tic game jumped, like, 200 percent.

■ **Extra toilet paper.** Always keep that secret stash somewhere in
your bathroom or house, usually in a closet or under the sink. You
don't ever want to use it, but wow, being without it, especially if you
have guests, is going to suck.

■ **Buy decent furniture.** By this I mean at a certain point you want
to invest in your furniture. It's okay to have some grungy couch
you've had since you were twenty, but eventually you'll want to buy
something nice and modern. I saved up to buy my first nice couch,
and I've had it more than four years. I hope to have it for even longer. Same goes with a recent chair purchase. It'll be in my life a
long time, so I want it to last.

■ **Buy shit that matches.** For each area of your home, you want everything in it to somewhat match. In your kitchen, try to have matching silverware and matching towels. In your living room, have the furniture be somewhat in the same style. In your bedroom, have your sheets go together. If, like me, you know nothing about style, it's okay to ask friends with smarter design instincts to help. Such as this one basic rule even I know: If you use any accent colors, it should appear three times in one area.

■ **Clean up.** Don't have your place be a mess, so regularly tidy up your home. Also, you don't want your place to look cluttered. The more shit you have lying around, the more it interacts with your brain. Studies show that homes with more clutter have more-stressed-out people. For me, cleaning up and making my place look de-cluttered is a stress reliever. It makes me think, "If I die right now, at least the people who find my body will think I was clean." (Mental note: Also, like your parents said, make sure when you die you're wearing clean underwear.)

Your goal is to make your place nice enough that you want to spend time in it *and* invite people over occasionally for nachos. (Always have nachos at your parties.) Not everyone is born understanding style (I certainly wasn't). You slowly figure it out, and you discover what you like and hate. (I hate wicker anything. Pottery Barn is where my soul goes to die.)

Your tastes also change over time. A chair you loved can now be something you despise. (Looking at you, Ikea chair from 2009.) So it's okay to get rid of things when they no longer fit your master style plan, if you even have one.

Also, not everything needs to be expensive. Check shops that resell furniture, or check Craigslist for deals in your area. (Except a mattress: Good Lord, never buy a mattress through Craigslist, someone was probably murdered on it.)

Regardless of where you end up in your life, usually your furniture and decorations come with you. So invest wisely. You want these items around for a while.

> **_Pro Tip:_** *The only people who should display the movie poster for* The Hangover *in their homes are cast members (speaking roles only).*

Don't Avoid Chores— Gamify Them

WHEN I WAS A WEE BOY, MY SISTER TRICKED ME INTO PICKING UP
sticks that had fallen off the tree in our backyard. She told me we
were going to play a game. Whoever picked up the most sticks won.
Guess who wanted to win? Me.

I picked up a boatload of sticks. My whole goal was to beat the
shit out of her, my older sister, who thought she knew everything,
who thought she was so cool with her ability to legally drive and
stay up late. After a few minutes, the backyard was clear of sticks.
I had the most. I kicked her ass. I won. Only years later did I realize she did this to me, over and over again, getting me to do my
chores secretly against my will. Because she turned chores from
being something awful into a game.

That's what most of your life is, just boring-ass chores. But if you
turn them into a game, you can make them fun. Here's an example
of how I can do that with buying groceries.

■ **Find a way that you can score yourself.** This could be something as simple as timing yourself, or using some other number-
based indicator: Can I find the string cheese in under two minutes?
Can I grab the wheat bread in less than fifty steps? What's the
cheapest I can make this trip?

■ **Did I get a higher score than last time?** Track this shit in your
phone, using a simple notes app: The last time I came to the store,
I took thirty minutes to buy everything; that means this time I
gotta try to beat thirty minutes this time.

■ **Can I listen to a podcast while doing it?** Usually, yes, I can. So now, not only am I trying to win this game I've created, I'm also being entertained in my ears. Good all around.

Here are a few examples of chores you can gamify:

■ Cleaning anything (Can you clean faster than last time? Only time will tell!)

■ Grocery shopping (Can you manage to buy everything on your list and keep it under a certain dollar amount? Coupons to the rescue!)

■ Laundry (Can you keep a streak alive of doing your laundry exactly every two weeks? Only you can prove it!)

■ Car maintenance (Can you manage to get your oil changed and *not* fall victim to the 293 other bullshit things your mechanic wants to charge you for? I bet you can!)

■ Figuring your budget (Can you save more money than last week? OMG, let's do it!)

Most of the bullshit you have to do in your life can be turned into a game. So now it's not a chore. It's something you've tricked your brain into thinking is fun. You'll be more likely to do it, and do it faster, if you're treating it that way. Game on, party pal.

Fun Fact: In college I used to do an after-hours chore game called "Drink the Remaining Beers in the Fridge." It led to another one: "Buy More Beer Tomorrow."

Create Something

IN MY EARLY TWENTIES, I QUIT MAKING MUSIC. EVER SINCE I WAS young, I'd either been taking piano lessons, singing in choirs, playing guitar and singing in shitty bands, performing in plays, or even playing trombone on funk albums. (Seriously, I did that once.) Instead I became completely focused on my career. It was all that mattered to me.

And I became miserable.

I truly believe a life where you create shit is better than one where you don't. Once I got into comedy, and writing for fun, and just creating for the sake of creating, I became less somber. Now I regularly write, perform, and create in my free time. Sure, sometimes I make embarrassing work—my mom regularly tells me my Twitter account keeps her from getting grandchildren from me—but at least I'm much more chipper these days.

All of our brains have a creative side, and if we don't let them have fun, they get pissed off. That's why you should have some sort of hobby where you're *making* shit. I don't mean you need to become a singer or a comedian or a poet, but you need to put your body and your mind together and create something that lives outside of you.

You could brew beer. Or knit hats. Or manage your recreational softball league. Or paint. Or stencil. Or sing torch songs. Or create an online comic. Or write monologue jokes on your blog. Or write young adult fiction. Or write midadult nonfiction advice books. Or do sketch comedy. Or create informative YouTube videos. Or start a podcast about dogs. Or make photos of your cat wearing fancy hats. Or create pottery. Or write poetry about the office. Or bake macaroons. Or design board games. Or build birdhouses. Or plant purple things in your garden. Or have a garden. Or write speed metal power anthems. Or learn ballroom dancing.

Just do something that's creative and outside your body. Because not only is it a stress reliever, it's a way of reaffirming you're alive and you matter.

With that, though, you need to know that for some of us, the act of creating can generate some stress and sadness. While writing this book, I hit drastic emotional bottoms. Self-doubt crept in every other week. (I edited out the dark parts, which involved copious eating of various cheeses.)

I now know that's normal. It's what can happen when you're stuck in your head, creating something out of thin air. While it can suck, I just needed to forge through. Eventually, I got better. The journey more than made up for the emotional rocks my creativity boat sometimes crashed on.

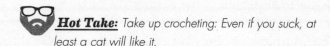 **_Hot Take:_** _Take up crocheting: Even if you suck, at least a cat will like it._

Never Read the Comments

THE MAJORITY OF THE INTERNET IS A CESSPOOL OF POINTLESSNESS that shouldn't be read by anyone. Other than that, it's not too bad. I've been a denizen of the Web since I was about ten or eleven. We got a free CD in the mail from AOL and installed it right quick. (Or maybe it was a floppy disk. I'm old.)

It didn't take long before someone was an asshole to me from the anonymity of their computer screen. I was in a chat room dedicated to Nintendo video games. A conversation was happening in front of me about how cool Star Wars was. I chimed in.

"Star Wars is AWESOME!" I typed. Others agreed. I'd found a group of people who were kind and liked the same things I did!

Then my first troll attacked.

A random guy in the chat room instant-messaged me. "Star Wars SUCKS!" he wrote. "That means YOU SUCK."

Almost two decades later, that sort of behavior is standard Internet communication. People think things suck. Or they think you suck. Then they tell you about it. Usually they won't shut up about it, writing further blog posts about how you're the Worst, or finding you on different social media platforms, just to further let you know you are Really the Worst. They will find anything in your life you've ever done to justify their beliefs, to cement their impression of you as Not Good and the things you say or do are Bad Bad Bad.

It's at the bottom of every well-edited article or blog post, or anything really: anonymous haters hating because haters gonna hate hate hate. They show up to be racist, sexist, just full of hatred.

Because of this awfulness, let's make a pledge right now: Let's not read the comments. They were a great idea. But most places do them so poorly that it's not worth it.

Don't join in. Trust that instinct. Manage your brain. Don't try to be a hero. Just don't read the comments.

> *Let's make a pledge right now: Let's not read the comments.*

Pro Tip: *The only time you should read the comments is if they were left by your mom. And your mom's not on Reddit.*

How to Get More Time in Your Life

EVER FIND YOURSELF COMPLAINING THERE JUST AREN'T ENOUGH hours in the day to get shit done? Well, you're probably spending a lot of time doing things that aren't exactly the best use of your life, without even realizing it. If you're truly wondering where your time goes, create a log where you track what you do every fifteen minutes of your day.

If you can't figure out what to cut, here are some ideas:

1. Watch less television

If you're ever flipping through channels, that means you're just trying to find something to waste your time. If you're doing that, stop and get up and do literally anything else. Kapow. Now you've got more time.

2. Watch less live sports

A basketball game lasts, on average, about two hours. A football game lasts a little more than three hours, on average. And each baseball game lasts, according to research by scientists, an average of 221 hours. Stop watching sports and you'll have so much more time.

3. Get rid of Netflix/Hulu/etc.

Think of the last TV show you binged all the way through. That's about twenty hours of your life you'll never get back. If you don't have any streaming services, you can't binge. I often find myself going to Netflix out of habit and searching half an hour for something to watch. That's just as bad as flipping aimlessly through channels.

4. Turn your notifications off

Every time you get a beep on your phone it causes you to break concentration and focus on something else. Whether it's a new Snapchat, a Facebook message, or a like from your crush on Instagram, it pauses you from whatever you were doing and causes you to waste time. If you're not receiving any notifications, you dip into apps by choice, not by default.

5. Stop checking your e-mail every five seconds

If something is superimportant, you'll get a phone call about it. Check your e-mail only every few hours. If you're off the clock, don't check it at all.

6. Go to the bar less

Lots of times you go to the bar to watch sports. Or just to kill time. Instead, do literally anything else.

7. Get more sleep

The more sleep you get, the more refreshed you'll feel and the more you'll want to use the valuable hours remaining in the day.

8. Stop endlessly scrolling on social media

If you get on your phone, open up your InstaFaceTweet app, and realize you're just scrolling for the sake of scrolling, put the phone down and do literally anything else. These apps pay big bucks to have people design them so you become addicted and keep scrolling forever, because that helps them make more money off your eyeballs. Put your eyeballs elsewhere.

9. Make a schedule

I know people who have every thirty-minute chunk of their day planned in their digital calendars. From work to bathroom breaks (wow) to exercise to phone calls to food—everything. It's all planned out. So by the time they're done with their day, they've got a huge chunk of time left for "do whatever." That's time they can use for anything else they want. But guess what they do when they figure out what goes in the "do whatever" spot? They fill that space in their calendar.

10. Eat more kale

It seems to fix everything else.

> **Pro Tip:** *If you want even more time in your life, invent time travel. Then go to 2004 and tell me not to grow that goatee.*

Stop Saying "Adulting"

I HATE IT WHEN PEOPLE USE THE TERM "ADULTING" OR SAY WHAT they're doing is "OMG, so adult right now!" This makes it seem as though what you're doing during the rest of your life is *not* being an adult. Or rather, that that time is somehow *lesser*. So in doing that underbrag about going to the grocery store or getting your new driver's license, or whatever standard adult chore you have to do, you diminish the normality of your life by making it seem as though you're not succeeding otherwise.

You're doing great. Even when you're not "acting" like an adult, it's okay, because you actively are one. Nobody is doing this shit perfectly. Not you, not me, not Jay Z, nobody. (Well, maybe Beyoncé.) We're all just making it up as we go.

> **Hot Take:** I can't wait for my generation to get into their seventies and start bragging on Twitter: "lol just broke my hip I'm eldering so hard rn."

Stop Saying "Hipster"

YEAH, I KNOW, A GUY WITH A BEARD AND BLACK-FRAMED GLASSES is telling you to stop using this word. But hear me out. Generally, when people use this word, it's for two reasons:

1. They don't like someone's fashion.
2. They think someone is pretentious.

If you don't like other people's fashion choices, who gives a shit? It doesn't impact your life, unless you run a clothing boutique and no one will shop there. Furthermore, what has been called "hipster" fashion has changed twenty times in my life. When I wore lots of plaid to hide how fat I was, I was called a hipster for wearing plaid. Now that I'm skinnier and I wear V-neck shirts because I'm vain and want to show off my arm cannons, I'm also a hipster. This means calling someone a hipster because of their clothing translates as, "That person looks cool and I have a problem with it." Stop giving a shit about how cool someone else dresses. I mean, really, my fellow cool people have had enough.

If you call people hipsters because you think they're pretentious, or that they think they're better than you because they have tastes or opinions different from yours, that's just another term for assholes. So don't call them hipsters. Call them assholes. But before you do that—are you *sure* they're being pretentious? Or are you throwing that veil on them because they just look or act differently from you? Wow, who's being pretentious now? That would be you.

Stop calling people hipsters. Instead, call them assholes. But only if they actually are. (And probably not to their faces. Because, again, it doesn't matter. Also because assholes will probably punch you.)

Hot Take: *Telling you not to use the word "hipster" automatically means you're allowed to call me one. God damn it.*

Which Advice Is Worth Taking

NOT ALL ADVICE IS WORTH TAKING, AND LEARNING WHEN YOU should take it is a skill that takes years to learn. Thankfully, you are reading a whole book filled with the greatest advice that's ever been bestowed upon humanity, so I know exactly what advice is worth taking (all of mine) and which is worth ignoring (everyone else's).

I kid. But really, the best advice is the kind that's actionable. Let's say you're getting a performance review at work. One of the things you hear is that, while you're good at communicating, sometimes your boss wishes you'd check in more on projects you're working on. That's something you can take action on: You now know you should be giving your boss more regular updates on your projects. So now you can set a calendar reminder to chat with with your boss every two or three days on a project. Easy fix.

But if your performance review just says "needs work," well, that's not exactly advice you can take action on. How are you going to "needs work" better? Or how can you tone it down? Who knows. So that's probably something that's actually trying to get at something else. So ask your boss to explain it more clearly.

Advice can also be more worthwhile depending on who it's from. If it's from someone in your field, and they're criticizing your work, that's better. If it's from a random stranger on Twitter whose avatar is an egg, it's probably not worthwhile. Anonymous advice is usually worthless. But advice attached to a name means that person's willing not only

> *Anonymous advice is usually worthless.*

to share his or her thoughts about you with you, but also to be held accountable for those thoughts. So it means the person usually puts more effort into those comments.

Advice that's actually meant to make you feel like shit isn't generally worth anything, either. Sometimes someone will "give you advice," when they actually are jealous or spiteful of you, and they want to make you feel bad or doubt yourself. This kind of advice will be filled with a lot of backhanded compliments—"For you, that's real good work!" or "I didn't know you were capable of doing something that competent!" or "I'm used to you doing poorly, but this isn't bad!"

That sort of shit is just meant to undermine you and hurt your feelings, so those people can piss off and you can ignore what they're saying. When it comes to advice, think back on this: Are they trying to actually help me get better? Can I take action based on what they said? If the answer is yes to both, then do it. Otherwise, forget it.

Pro Tip: *Advice is like meth. Just because someone from your hometown gives it to you doesn't mean you should take it.*

You Should Read More

ONE OF THE BEST THINGS MY PARENTS DID FOR ME WAS GETTING ME hooked on reading at a young age. I would read on car rides. I would read on vacations. I would read in the bleachers while my hometown's high school won the girls' state basketball championship. (I know, I'm very cool.)

I owe most of my success to this: I read as often as I can. I think I'm able to solve problems because I've read about so many different things. Fiction, nonfiction, pornographic romance novels about cowboys and countesses—everything you read exposes you (lol) to new situations and shows you how different choices play out, for better or worse. (Just so we're clear, I like my pornographic romance novels to be about vampires.)

You should probably read more. I mean, I know, you're reading this book, which is a great first step. Please buy twenty-five copies for all your friends, and then tell them to buy twenty-five copies for their friends. But outside of this book, you should be spending a lot of your free time reading.

■ **First of all, it's sexy as hell.** Whenever I show up to someone's house and they've got a lot of books on their shelves, I know this is a person I want to talk to. John Waters, the famed filmmaker and mustache-haver, had a great quote on the subject: "If you go home with someone and they don't have books, don't fuck them."

■ **It teaches you shit.** Even if you're *not* reading how-to books or memoirs of people who've lived fantastical lives, just by reading anything you're learning about *something*. (Sometimes you learn about the lives of teenage vampires!)

■ **It teaches you more about the human condition.** Most books, other than probably math or science textbooks, contain humans doing shit. Usually, these people get into conflicts and something happens. (Unless it's a superboring literary tome where they just describe how pretty the fucking sunset is and not a goddamn thing happens other than people are mopey and sad.)

■ **The more you read, the better you communicate.** You develop a better vocabulary and a better grasp of language when you read great writing. You also learn from reading shitty writing, because it tells you, "Oh, my God, I do not want to talk or write like this." (I'm sure reading this book has taught you lots about shitty writing.)

■ **It's relaxing.** Jumping into a magical world you get to invent while reading is amazing. You tend to forget about your own struggles, the issues you're dealing with that day. You're transported into a new place. Books are easily the cheapest form of escapism.

It's the ultimate in alone time, because you're stuck in your brain with only yourself, making words come alive. Speaking of coming alive, don't read any apocalyptic zombie novels before you go to bed. Because then you'll feel the need not only to sleep with the lights on, but also to build a contraption that makes noise if anyone walks toward your room. And you'll think a zombie is coming to kill you, but nope, just your asshole cat. *The power of literature!*

Who Knew: *Here's a great pickup line: "Hey, girl, are you a David Foster Wallace book? Because everyone says you're great but I can't understand you." Also, don't use pickup lines.*

Random Advice in Convenient List Form

1. Drink more water.
2. The best way to take a compliment from a friend is by smiling and simply saying, "Thank you."
3. Drink less booze, probably.
4. It's okay if you don't like [insert popular TV show or movie]. Being different is what makes you you.
5. Clean your bathtub at least once a month.
6. Don't send an e-mail while you're still angry.
7. Nothing great happens because of a text sent between two and five a.m.
8. Eat more green things, preferably vegetables.
9. Eat less sugar.
10. It's okay to stay in for the weekend and go to bed early.
11. Wear sunscreen more often.
12. It's okay to be scared.
13. You're not defined by your past mistakes unless you purposefully don't learn from them.
14. Leave your regular surroundings on occasion and explore someplace new.
15. If someone invites you to go do something and you have no plans, try to say yes and enjoy the adventure.
16. You're not always right, so if many people you respect tell you you're wrong, think about why that is.
17. Always try learning something new.

18. When in doubt, ask someone for help.

19. No one was born amazingly talented, and neither were you. Practice and you'll get better.

20. Try to always dress as if you'll be meeting the love of your life later. Because you might.

21. Give more in everything than you receive, because it somehow ends up giving you even more.

22. What you do for work doesn't define you unless you let it.

23. Your boss is not your parent, so don't expect them to fill that role for you. Don't ask them to help you change a tire on your car, because they will stare at you stone-faced and then you will walk away slowly, having embarrassed you both.

24. Reread every e-mail before you send it.

25. Just because someone is different from you doesn't mean they're a bad person.

26. Go look at art.

27. Someday you will die. Is it really worth staying mad at someone forever?

28. Everyone's got their own quirks, just like you, so don't judge them for it.

29. When you make a mistake, own up to it quickly and figure out how to learn from it.

30. Bragging about your salary is usually awful. So don't do it.

31. You probably own more stuff than you need, so before buying anything, ask yourself if you truly need it.

32. Twix is better than Snickers, but Butterfinger is better than both.

33. When in doubt about what you should do in a situation, choose the option that is the kindest toward the largest group of people.

34. Stretch more.

35. It's okay to occasionally pig out and eat a bunch of food. Just don't do it all the time.

36. You get to decide what success means for you, not someone else. You're living your own life, not theirs.

37. You never have to do something if someone double-doggy dares you, especially if it involves dog poop.

Some Final Thoughts

AS I WRITE THIS, I'M THIRTY. I'M ABOUT A THIRD DONE WITH MY
life. I'm aware I barely know a goddamn thing. But despite that, I
know these are the two most important things in life:

1. Believe in others.
2. Believe in yourself.

I like to take long walks in Chicago. If you've never been, come
visit. Chicago's the greatest city in the world, according to everyone whose opinions matter (like mine). Just trust me on this: I don't
have a passport and one time I drove to Canada when you could
still just drive to Canada, so I think I know what I'm talking about.

The city has its problems, sure. Crime, institutional racism,
Wrigleyville. Awful things created by people, perpetuated by people, enforced by people. But during my walks, I see amazing things
every time. Folks helping strangers by holding open doors, changing tires, walking elderly people across the street.

I see people hugging people, playing with dogs in the parks,
punk rockers in coffee shops sitting next to moms in yoga pants
and men in pinstriped suits, all enjoying chai tea lattes. People of
different backgrounds and lifestyles, getting along relatively well,
at least relative to the history of human civilization.

One time an old family friend was in town and I was showing
her around. She asked me what my favorite place was in the city.
The sun was setting, so I knew where to go. We walked west toward the North Avenue bridge. From that point, facing south, you
can see the entire beautiful skyline of downtown Chicago. My favorite view in the whole world.

"Why do you like this spot so much?" she asked.

"Because," I said, "this view wouldn't have happened unless tens of thousands of people came together to create it. They had to make thousands, if not millions, of tiny decisions. They had to compromise and agree, for more than a hundred years, to design and build those tall buildings. So whenever I look toward them, it gives me hope that we can do anything."

Growing up, I used to think humanity was majority bad. Our history would make you think that. Despite all that we've managed to destroy, we've created a lot, too. And continue to create. None of that happens in a vacuum. Every wonderful thing happened because people believed in one another, or in just one person, and that made it a reality. We're all standing on one another's shoulders, succeeding together.

Speaking of success, I was fortunate to discover the punk rock ethos when I was younger. While the music (and fashion!) is an amalgamation of things, the idea of punk rock is simple: You don't need anyone's permission to just go out and do shit.

It told me if you want to start a band, you get people together and do it. Who cares if you suck at your instruments? Write some songs. Get booked at some venues, or, better yet, create your own place to play shows. You aren't ever beholden to existing power structures. Just do your own damn thing because you want to do it and you can.

Part of what makes that ethos a success is believing in yourself. That's why you're able to have success: You just decide you're going to try your damnedest and keep going. My entire life has followed that, whether I knew it or not.

Why does someone become a journalist? Because they believe in themselves. Why does someone become an accountant? Because they believe in themselves. Why does someone become a parent? Because they believe in themselves. (Also, usually, sex.)

One of the biggest problems I see is people who lack that belief in themselves. Some of it is societal. Some of it is because of how they were raised. I know I'm privileged as hell, and part of that was being raised with even the notion of believing in myself. But even if you weren't, you just need to start telling yourself these simple words: I believe in you.

Say this out loud right now to yourself in a mirror: I believe in you.

Doesn't that feel better? I say those magic words to myself all the time. But also to everyone else. A friend of mine would always tell me he believed in me whenever we saw each other. Every time he said it to me, it filled me with so much hope. So I started saying it to other people. And to myself.

■ ■ ■

That's all I have to say. I hope this book was helpful. It certainly was helpful for me to write it. So yeah.

Good luck.

I believe in you.

—ANDY BOYLE
Dictated and read

Acknowledgments

DEEP THANKS TO MY EDITOR, MARIAN LIZZI. NOT ONLY DID SHE HELP
clear up my clutter and make this book funnier, she's also the one
who asked me to write it. Thank you thank you thank you. And
thanks to everyone else at TarcherPerigee who helped make this a
reality.

Very special thanks to Noah Ballard, my agent, who was a fantastic copilot for this project. He held my hand and kept me (mostly)
from looking like a dumbass. I'm glad I'm less of an asshole now
than when we met in college.

My friends Emily Greenhalgh, Holly Leach, and others who
asked not to be named were the book's first readers. Their comments pushed the book to be better than I could make it, and their
constant encouragement made writing it so much easier. Y'all
rule. Especially Emily, who made this book funnier.

Thanks to my former colleagues at the *Chicago Tribune*, Marcia
Lythcott and Lara Weber, who were kind enough to run my piece
on not drinking in the newspaper, minus the swears, which helped
make this book happen. And thanks to Kurt Gessler for getting
them interested in it. And to all the media outlets who reran it, or
put me on TV or the radio because of it. Thanks for helping me to
get recognized randomly in public.

I'm a funnier person for having known and created silliness
with my friends Mel and Josh, so thanks to those two goofs. Thanks
to Terrance Brown, who helped me complete my first screenplay,
proving to me I could actually *finish* something creative. Thanks to
the thousands of other creative people I've shared stages with, took

classes with, or collaborated with, or who, by being supremely talented in front of me, just allowed me to glean a trick or seven and make myself better.

Definite thanks to my coworkers, past and present, especially the folks at the NBC News and Breaking News (RIP) family. Thanks for being supportive when I went viral and had to take days off to go be on television (humblebrag).

I couldn't have finished this book without the love and support of my family (Mama Patti, Father Steve, Sister Cindy, Bro-in-Law Kent, and the little ones, Maddie and Alex). I also am grateful for my friends, who kept me sane during the writing of this, as well as everyone else on the Internet (strangers, mild acquaintances, secret enemies) who pushed me forward. You're all so wonderful. Thanks for existing.

My continued gratitude to everyone who's dealt with me when I've been a mild jerk, a raging piece of shit, a notorious asshole. Many people in my personal, educational, and professional worlds have been patient with me while I was, shall we say, not striving for the heights of my potential. All the people who've pushed me to be better than I wanted to be, especially when I didn't want to change, are the real heroes here. Thank you in advance for not writing your own tell-alls about how I used to be more of a dick.

I'd like to thank Nickelback and their fans for making me reevaluate how I judge everyone and leading me down a more positive path. Without Nickelback, I wouldn't be where I am today, which was an interesting sentence to type.

Lastly, thank you, dearest reader. By reading this book it means you're trying to improve yourself, which will (hopefully) make the world a better place. Unless you're one of those weirdos who buys books just to read the acknowledgments. In that case, thanks for your money and please buy twenty more copies!

About the Author

Andy Boyle is a comedian, writer, and Internet maker. He is definitely a human man and not three stacked children inside a trench coat. Originally from Nebraska, for the last decade he's worked for many media outlets, including NBC News, the *Chicago Tribune*, the *Boston Globe*, and the *New York Times* Regional Media Group, where his work with the *Tuscaloosa News* was cited in the 2012 Pulitzer Prize for Breaking News. He is six foot two, so there's no way he's two full-grown Siberian huskies on each other's shoulders while wearing rain gear, either, as that would be too short. As of this writing, Andy's been a college instructor, a terrible improv coach, an unpaid screenwriter, a paid copywriter, a barely paid stand-up comedian, an essayist for money, a host of a Web series for negative money, and the undisputed favorite son of his parents. He is also assuredly neither a swarm of bees nor a pit of snakes somehow holding up a London Fog overcoat. Andy regularly does talks and things into microphones throughout the United States, and sometimes people laugh on purpose. In his alleged free time he lifts weights and plays with his cat, Tiberius, who pooped in the bathtub while this paragraph was written. He lives in Chicago, and no matter what the rumors say, he's definitely, 100 percent, a human.

To book Andy to talk somewhere or to write something, please visit AndyBoyle.com. His parents want you to follow him on Twitter @andymboyle.